Emotional Intelligence

Managing emotions to make a positive impact on your life

Second Edition

Gill Hasson

CAPSTONE
A Wiley Brand

Registered Office(s)

John Wiley & Sons, Inc., 111 River Street, Hoboken, NJ 07030, USA
John Wiley & Sons Ltd, The Atrium, Southern Gate, Chichester, West Sussex, PO19 8SQ, UK

For details of our global editorial offices, customer services, and more information about Wiley products visit us at www.wiley.com.

Library of Congress Cataloging-in-Publication Data is Available:

ISBN 9781907312632 (Paperback)
ISBN 9781907312670 (ePub)
ISBN 9781907312687 (ePDF)

Cover Design: Wiley
Cover Image: © VVadi4ka/Adobe Stock

Set in 11/14 pt and Sabon LT Std by Straive, Chennai, India
SKY10086082_093024

For Alba, Oscar, Robin and Jacob.

Contents

Introduction

What is emotional intelligence?

What is emotional intelligence? It's being intelligent with your emotions.

Emotional intelligence is the ability to both understand *and* manage emotions.

It's using your emotions to inform your thinking and using your thinking to understand and manage emotions.

Although regular intelligence – the ability to reason, rationalise, analyse and so on – is important in life, emotional intelligence is the key to thinking clearly and creatively, to being able to manage stress and challenges confidently and relate well to others.

In this book you will learn how to understand and manage your emotions – your own and other people's – in a way that is helpful and can make a real, positive difference to your life.

Understanding emotions

Emotions are part of being human. Whether we're aware of them or not, emotions are a constant presence in our lives, influencing everything we do. Emotions are the glue that connects us to other people and gives meaning to our lives.

Emotions cause us to feel, think and act in different ways in different situations. But emotions can be complicated. This can make them hard to understand; difficult to make sense of and take meaning from.

Understanding emotions involves:

- recognising and understanding the three aspects of emotions – physical states, thoughts and actions – and how they interact;
- being aware of the differences, transition, variations and degrees of intensity between emotions;
- understanding what, how and why you and other people experience certain emotions in certain situations.

Chapter 1 starts you on the road to understanding emotions by looking at the nature of emotions – the inherent aspects of emotions: what all emotions have got in common.

You will see that emotions are made up of three parts: thoughts, physical feelings and behaviour. Any one part of an emotion can trigger and influence another part.

Take, for example, anxiety. Supposing you were anxious about an exam, an interview or a social occasion. Anxiety might start with a thought ('I'm dreading this'), which might trigger physical feelings (stomach turns over, tense muscles, dry mouth) and then behaviour (unable to sit still or relax).

But your anxiety could start with the physical feeling of dread (stomach turning over, etc.), which reminds you of and makes you think about the upcoming exam or social event ('I'm dreading this'), which results in the behaviour of pacing up and down. And, of course, the anxiety could start with the inability to relax which triggers the physical feelings and the thoughts that go with them.

No wonder we so often struggle to understand and manage emotions! Although we do see some emotions as positive, there are plenty of other emotions that we regard as 'negative' or 'wrong'.

However, as you develop your understanding of what, exactly, emotions are and why we have them, you will see that judging emotions as 'positive' or 'negative', 'good' or 'bad' isn't very helpful.

The fact is, *all* emotions have a positive purpose – to keep you safe, to help you make decisions, to develop and maintain social bonds, to experience happiness and creative processes. You can read more about the positive intent of emotions in Chapter 1.

Chapter 2 helps further your understanding by looking at *specific* emotions; their levels of intensity, the differences and similarities between them and the relationships between them.

Understanding, for example, what envy and jealousy are: envy is wanting to have something that someone else has got – to feel envy when someone you know gets a promotion. Jealousy on the other hand, is a feeling of *resentment* that another has gained something that you think you more rightfully deserve: feeling jealous of a promotion that you feel *you* should have received instead of the other person. Knowing the difference between those two emotions can help you have a clearer picture of what you're feeling and why.

You will learn that disentangling what *triggers* an emotion from the thoughts, feelings and behaviour that are part of it can also help you to understand the emotion – and see it as 'just emotion', rather than getting caught up and over-whelmed by it.

Of course, although we all feel and experience emotions, an important part of emotional intelligence is understanding and accepting that emotions are experienced differently by different people. Not only that, different people have different ideas and beliefs about emotions – their purpose and intent and how to respond to them.

Understanding this helps you to start managing other people and their emotions more effectively.

Managing emotions

Once you have a clearer understanding of the nature and purpose of emotions, you are in a better position to manage them.

In Chapter 3 you will learn that managing emotions means drawing on emotions to inform your thinking, reasoning and behaviour.

Managing emotions includes the following:

- Knowing when to respond immediately and when to stop and think.

- Knowing when to rein in your emotions; when to engage or detach from an emotion.
- Knowing what is, in any one situation, an appropriate and inappropriate expression of emotion – in yourself and in other people.
- Being able to manage other people's emotions.
- Knowing how to draw on emotions to develop empathy and rapport with others.

People with good levels of emotional intelligence know that managing emotions does not mean controlling them; it doesn't involve dominating or suppressing emotions. Instead, managing emotions involves being flexible with your thinking, behaviour and responses; being able to stay open to feelings, both those that are pleasant and those that are unpleasant.

And because we all experience and respond to emotions in different ways, Chapter 3 suggests a *range* of strategies and responses to manage emotions, other people, events and situations. The emphasis is on identifying ways that work for you, personally, to manage emotions and the thoughts, feelings and behaviour that go with them.

By the end of Part 1, you will have understood, then, that emotional intelligence involves both understanding and managing emotions – yours and other people's.

It's a dynamic process; the extent to which you can understand and manage your own emotions influences your ability to understand and manage other people's emotions. And vice versa.

However, emotional intelligence is not limited to specific strategies to manage specific emotions, people and situations.

There is further scope for you to understand and manage emotions – yours and other people's.

Communication skills, assertiveness, a positive approach and an optimistic outlook are key features of emotional intelligence.

In Part 2 we start by looking at how you can develop your emotional intelligence by developing your communication skills.

You will learn that good communication is an inherent part – a permanent and inseparable element – of emotional intelligence. How come?

Communication between people involves expressing thoughts, ideas, opinions, feelings and emotions. It involves making sense and meaning; understanding each other, what we each think and feel. And we all know how hard that can often be!

Chapter 4 will help you become a better communicator – it will give you insights, ideas and plenty of tips and techniques on how to 'read between the lines' and get a better understanding of what others are thinking and feeling.

It's not difficult – you simply draw on the natural ability we all already have to understand someone else's experience, their point of view, their thoughts and feelings. Even when their experience, perspective and feelings differ from your own.

This ability is called empathy. And while we all have the ability to empathise, it's an ability that can be improved in easy, straightforward ways. How? Simply by observing, listening and asking questions.

How, though, you might ask, can you better express *your* thoughts, opinions, feelings and emotions? By knowing how to assert yourself. Again, assertiveness is an integral part of emotional intelligence. Chapter 5 explains that just as emotional intelligence involves being able to understand and manage your feelings, so does being assertive.

Assertiveness calls for you to express thoughts, opinions and feelings in direct, honest and appropriate ways while at the same time taking into consideration the other person's opinions, feelings and needs.

Again, this chapter has plenty of advice and easy to follow techniques that you can use to help you to be more assertive. Don't worry if the thought of saying what you feel, think, want and don't want makes you anxious; I encourage you to start small and explain how you can practise being assertive in low-stakes situations. Once you feel comfortable in these low-risk situations, you will feel more confident to move on to other issues and situations, little by little.

And as your confidence improves, so will your emotional intelligence.

Good emotional intelligence, like all skills, is also helped if supported with a confident, positive approach and attitude. Having a positive outlook does not mean ignoring or suppressing difficult emotions or ignoring the challenging aspects of life. Chapter 6 explains that positive thinking allows you to approach difficult emotions and situations in an appropriate, helpful way.

With a positive approach, you acknowledge feelings such as jealousy, disappointment, guilt and so on, but rather than let them drag you down into a spiral of negative thinking, you know that these emotions have positive intentions. You know that events, other people, yourself and your emotions can be better managed with a positive attitude.

In fact, you even find that as a result of a positive mindset difficult emotions like regret, irritation, frustration and disappointment are less intense and make fewer appearances! You see life as filled with possibilities and solutions instead of worries and difficulties.

In Part 3, we turn to specific situations where emotional intelligence can make a big difference to the outcome.

These situations include occasions when you experience and need to manage anxiety, anger or disappointment. I also explain how to manage and support someone else who is struggling with these feelings.

You will get a better understanding of emotions such as anxiety and worry, disappointment and anger. You'll notice that the same features of emotional intelligence – assertive communication and positive thinking – arise throughout.

Often, difficult emotions are managed by sticking with one emotional response, whatever the situation is.

However, our emotions control us when we assume there's only *one* way to react. You will see we have a choice – we can identify and use strategies that work for each one of us according to the situation, other people and so on.

Emotional intelligence is not only about understanding and managing *difficult* emotions. The last chapter of this book focuses on engaging the 'feel good' emotions that motivate and inspire people.

When there's a specific goal that you want someone to achieve – or they themselves want to achieve – you need to *motivate* them. Motivation is what prompts and drives us to do and achieve something.

When you want to spark and enthuse someone to do something, you need to *inspire* them. Inspiration is what fills a person with an animating, exciting influence.

Whether you want to motivate or inspire, the emphasis is on engaging their heads and their hearts; their logic, reasoning, imaginations and emotions. Chapter 11 explains how to do this.

Why emotional intelligence matters

Understanding and managing others' emotions is essential to your social wellbeing; your interactions and relationships with other people. The ability to pick up on and respond to others' emotions in appropriate ways can help you to live and work with others more easily.

Understanding and managing your own emotions is essential to your *personal* wellbeing; your mental and physical health.

It's easy for many of us, with so many competing demands and commitments, to feel overwhelmed with life; to spin into confusion, isolation and negativity. Improve your emotional intelligence and you improve your ability to understand and manage your emotions. You can think more clearly and creatively; manage stress and challenges, communicate more easily with others; and display trust, empathy and confidence.

Better emotional intelligence – understanding and managing emotions – can help you to lead a happier life because acting rationally and calmly in difficult situations can, in time, become second nature.

You will be in a better position to handle a range of circumstances, events and other people that in the past you've found difficult or stressful.

By understanding your emotions and how to manage them, you're better able to express how you feel, what you want and don't want, while at the same time acknowledging and understanding how others may be feeling. This allows you to communicate more effectively; to talk with and understand others and forge stronger relationships, both in your personal life and at work.

Emotional intelligence at work

You've probably noticed that it's not the smartest people that are the most successful or the most fulfilled in life. You've probably noticed that being clever, talented or skilled is not enough. How well you do in your career may well depend on how well you get on with your colleagues, manager and clients.

Experience or qualifications might get you the job, but it's your ability to manage other people and your interactions with them that will keep you there and enable you to enjoy and progress in your work.

Emotional intelligence can help you manage office politics and navigate the social complexities of the workplace. And when you've cracked that nut, you're well positioned to manage a range of social situations!

Be patient with yourself as you learn to improve your emotional intelligence. As you read this book, simply pick out a few ideas, tips and techniques that appeal to you and try them out. Be prepared to take a few risks. If, despite your efforts and best intentions, a situation doesn't turn out as you had hoped, reflect on how you could respond differently in a similar situation next time.

That's being emotionally intelligent!

PART ONE
Understanding Emotions

1
What Emotions Are and Why We Have Them

Emotions are what move us. Emotions are a driving force. In any one day, a range of emotions can take you on a rollercoaster that brings you up and then takes you down.

You know how it is: in the morning a project is cancelled despite all the work you put into it. You feel frustrated and angry. But then a friend phones with some good news. You're delighted. There's a long queue for lunch. More frustration. Back at work you're told that the project is back on after all. Joy! Then your brother phones to say he and his wife have separated. You're sad and disappointed. A colleague announces she's got a promotion (you are envious and regret that you didn't apply for the job). But your son texts to say he got a part in the school play. You're pleased and happy.

The emotional rollercoaster takes you up high where the view is great but then it suddenly plunges you down, turning you upside down and rolling you around, before taking you up on a high again.

Nothing vivifies and nothing kills like the emotions.
Joseph Roux

What are emotions?

Emotions are an important part of being human; emotions cause us to feel, think and act in different ways – to do something or avoid doing something.

Emotions are complex reactions that engage our bodies and minds; they play an important role in how we think, feel and behave. In fact, any one emotion can be made up of thoughts, feelings and behaviour. Let's look at each of those aspects more closely.

Behavioural aspects

The behavioural aspect of an emotion is the most obvious, observable aspect. The behavioural aspects are concerned with how we respond to a situation; what we do or don't do, what actions we do or don't take. You can actually see the effect of the emotion in another person; you might, for example, see someone who is anxious wring and rub their hands. Someone else might tap their foot when irritated or impatient. Some of us bang the table with our fist when we are angry. Some people jump up and down when they are excited; when, for example, their team is winning.

Physical aspects

These are the physical changes: the internal bodily changes you experience – for example, increased heart rate, feeling queasy – when you experience an emotion.

When an emotion occurs, particularly a strong basic emotion like fear or anger, chemicals – hormones – secreted by the body's various glands are activated and spread to other parts of the body.

Your body's muscles, circulatory system, digestive system and organs such as your heart and liver shift from their normal level or function due to the effects of chemical and neural action.

Some of these physical responses can be observed, such as the constriction or dilation of the iris of your eyes, sweating and blushing. Other responses are relatively hidden, such as an increased heart rate, stomach activity and an increase or decrease in saliva.

Interestingly, some very different emotions provoke the same physical response. For example, excitement and anxiety can have the same sensations, such as rapid breathing and a pounding heart. In that case, what determines whether what you feel is happy or anxious? Your thoughts.

Cognitive aspects of emotions

Your thoughts – ideas, beliefs and mental images – are also part of an emotion.

For example, supposing you had an important interview, presentation or meeting tomorrow. Your thoughts might include: 'I don't know if I can do this – I might dry up and forget what to say.' You might get butterflies in your stomach; your heart rate increases and you start feeling hot.

In some ways, emotions are your thoughts felt physically; your thoughts can lead to a physical change.

Most women who have breastfed their child will tell you that they only had to *think* of their baby and they could feel milk come into their breasts. You don't, though, have to be nursing a baby to experience similar effects.

Imagine, for example, that you are given a big ripe juicy orange. Imagine yourself smelling the orange, feeling its texture, smelling its distinct citrus aroma. Next, see yourself cutting the orange into four quarters and taking one of those quarters and putting it into your mouth and taking a big juicy bite. If you imagined this clearly, you would notice that your mouth started to produce some extra saliva. You may have noticed your mouth puckering up and perhaps even watering.

Emotions are dynamic; any one aspect can trigger the other. How you think, feel and act are intrinsically linked.

If your computer has ever failed to do what you want, you may well have found yourself getting angry. Your angry response could begin with a *physical* reaction: a rise in adrenaline, rapid heart beat and breathing. This triggers a *behavioural* reaction: you thump the table. This is immediately followed by the *thought:* 'Oh my God! Now I won't get this work finished.'

Or, you could thump the table first. This could trigger a physical response: an adrenaline rush, rapid heart beat and breathing. Again, your thoughts follow close behind.

Or the angry response could begin with the thought: 'Oh my God! Now I won't get the work finished.' This thought triggers adrenaline, which increases your heart rate and affects your breathing.

Usually, we're not that aware of these different aspects of an emotion. Sometimes one aspect is so strong that it overwhelms and hides the other aspects. Other times, one aspect of an emotion may be so difficult that you automatically suppress that part. You might, for example, shut down or suppress uncomfortable thoughts.

The science of emotions

Feeling sad when a good friend moves away, anxiety before a test or exam, feeling thrilled that you've been offered the job, reacting with fear when you are watching a scary film – you might think you understand how you feel and what causes those feelings.

But just how is your brain influencing your emotions?

Your brain is made up of many different parts that all work together to process the information it receives. Emotional responses appear to come from one area of the brain: the amygdala; a small structure within the limbic system, one of the first areas in the human brain to develop.

The way the limbic system responds to experiences and situations is simple and basic. And because the limbic system regulates the emotions, your emotional responses are also simple and basic.

For example, even though another part of your brain can reason that when you're filled with fear watching a scary film, it is, in fact, *just* a film and you are not in danger, the limbic system cannot. It's not the thinking part of your brain. So, when you watch a scary movie and someone in that film is about to be attacked, you react automatically and immediately, without thinking.

So, the limbic system enables you to respond quickly, instinctively and without having to think about it. When you are in actual danger – if it is you that is being threatened with being attacked – you need to react quickly. There's no time to think, you need to move fast!

Another part of your brain – the neocortex – is the thinking, reasoning, part of your brain. The neocortex enables the most complex mental activity, such as conscious thought, language and spatial reasoning. However, it is much slower than the limbic system.

So if, for example, you suddenly see a car, snake, falling tree coming towards you, you're unlikely to use your neocortex to think through the potential danger – your limbic system will snap into action and make you react *without* thinking.

Rational thinking is sometimes too slow for handling a threat (a tree falling towards you). Sometimes, you need to react more quickly and basic emotions, like fear and surprise, help you do that. They are survival mechanisms and are hardwired into our biology, just like metabolic processes and muscle reflexes.

Intuition

Another example of the limbic system in action are the occasions when you have a split second's awareness – an 'inner voice' that tells you something in an instant.

If you've ever had a moment where you felt as though something wasn't right – when things didn't seem to add up – then you've experienced intuition. Conversely, you could've experienced situations where everything *did* add up; everything did seem to come together to tell you to take action straight away. That's also your intuition – an immediate knowing.

You don't know why – you just feel it. Intuition cuts out all the thought and leaps straight to the answer. Sometimes referred to as gut feeling, that gut feeling – or a hunch – presents itself to you as an immediate sensation. It is noticeable enough to be acted on, yet too quick for you to need to process and understand it.

Here's an example of intuition providing immediate knowledge.

Ruby was walking along a crowded beach in Spain with her three-year-old son Jack. Three local, middle-aged women were walking close by in the same direction. Every time her son stopped to examine a shell or pebble, the women slowed their pace. Ruby was only vaguely aware of this. At one point the women stopped abruptly in front of Ruby and Jack. Ruby bumped into them. She apologised and carried on walking with her son but was aware that the women had dispersed and walked off in different directions. Without thinking or knowing why, Ruby suddenly checked her bag. Her purse was gone. That immediate knowledge that something definitely wasn't right alerted her to take action. Ruby grabbed her son, ran after one of the women and started loudly remonstrating with her, accusing the woman of having stolen her purse. People around them stopped and stared and a nearby police officer began to approach the small crowd. Another of the women returned to the scene. Ruby felt a tug on her bag – she looked inside – her purse had been dropped back into her bag.

There's nothing mystical or coincidental about intuition; it's simply everything you subconsciously already know in certain circumstances, coming together at once. And to benefit from this knowledge – your intuition – you need to be aware of and tune in to what your senses are telling you; what your ears, eyes, nose, sense of taste and/or touch and the physical sensations are communicating to you. And you need to be aware of what past experience has taught you.

Everyone has intuition – it's a process that gives you the ability to know something directly without thinking. It bridges the gap between the conscious and unconscious parts of your mind, and between instinct and reason.

Intuitive messages are often keen and quick, which makes them easy to miss. So often, intuitive messages are drowned out by all the other internal and external noise and activity that is going on in and around you.

How to develop and hone your intuition

To begin, listen to your body and the signals it is giving. In any situation.

By being aware of your physical feelings in everyday situations, when, for example, something doesn't feel right, or you feel unsure about something, you will be more likely to recognise that your body is warning you against something.

Listen to what's going on around you. Listening is different from hearing. Hearing involves being aware of sound. Listening involves concentrating on sound.

Stop and notice some of the sounds around you right now: traffic, the wind in the trees or the birds outside; the sound of the TV, radio or someone talking in the next room; the sound of your breathing. Or the sound of silence.

It's not just what you hear that can alert you to what's going on. All your senses are constantly picking up information from the world around you. Be aware of what you see – take notice, for example, of the changing light throughout the day.

Be more aware of how things feel to the touch, notice the different smells in the air.

Being more aware of your environment – the sights, sounds, smells and so on – on an everyday basis will serve you well when the crucial messages need to get through. In a range of situations, when things seem out of place or unusual, you will recognise it's your intuition communicating with you.

In any situation, be open to *all* the messages your intuition is communicating. Rather than interpret a single signal (unless it is overwhelming – there's a strong smell of gas or smoke, the other person is clutching a weapon, a group of people are all looking extremely agitated), be alert for a combination of signals.

When that combination of messages your senses are receiving does add up, your intuition will come through loud and clear! You simply need to stay focused, ignore distractions and act fast!

The function of emotions

We've seen, then, that your brain functions to create the best response to a situation and it uses emotions as the catalyst to prompt you to act. Emotions move you. Literally.

There are three main areas where emotions are useful.

Physical safety value

As you've just read, emotions can prompt you to react quickly in response to danger. Emotions get your attention and demand a response; they motivate you to take action and keep safe.

It would appear that we have six basic emotions – fear, anger, disgust, surprise, sadness and joy. The main function of basic emotions like fear and disgust is to protect you. Disgust is an automatic response that we experience when, for example, we encounter something that could transmit disease and cause us to be unwell. Anger quickly transforms us into a state where we're ready to fight and fear can prompt us to flee from dangerous situations.

These emotions don't wait for you to think, to reason and to process what's going on. Instead, they instantly warn you of danger and get you to move out of harm's way immediately.

Social value
Basic emotions such as fear and anger may appear to be self-serving rather than altruistic. But emotions evolved not just to keep *you* safe, but to bind us together with others as we all have a better chance of surviving and thriving when we consider each other's needs, cooperate and live in harmony with each other.

Social emotions – also known as moral emotions – such as trust, guilt, gratitude, shame, compassion and love – enable us to live and work with each other. They regulate and guide our interactions; they allow us to initiate and maintain social ties and bonds that bring families, friends, neighbours and communities together.

To experience these emotions, you need empathy – an ability to understand how different circumstances and situations influence and impact each other. You need to be aware of how your behaviour would be received by other people; how you may be judged. For example, you may refrain from stealing because you know it will upset the other person and you will be judged as a 'bad' person – and may then be ostracised from your community.

Creative value

Creativity is the ability to create and express – through art, poetry, music and so on – ideas and thoughts.

When it comes to creativity, emotions are a double-edged sword. Emotions can inspire or hinder creativity. Anger can inspire a dramatic painting. Despair and sadness, for example, can paralyse creativity. But despair and sadness could (and do) inspire beautiful, moving poetry and songs. In turn, creative experiences can provoke and inspire emotions. A poem or film, for example, can move you to tears. So can a piece of music.

If you've ever sat in heavy traffic getting more and more frustrated only to find yourself perking up because a favourite tune just came on the radio, you'll know that music can completely change the way you feel. There's nothing like putting on your favourite song to lift your spirits. But music can also make you sad or fill you with determination.

Emotions, then, help keep you safe, help you establish and maintain connections with other people and inspire your creativity. Emotions can enhance and widen experience. Emotions can block and limit experience.

Positive and negative emotions: why are some emotions 'good' and others are 'bad'?

When you feel good, you tend to open up and reach out. This provides the basis for positive social interactions. Typically, you are more tolerant, more open to new ideas and new experiences. You feel more positive about situations and other people – generous and open to seeing possibilities.

Emotions that make you feel good can also motivate you to repeat an action or experience; the experience of joy is a pleasurable one, and motivates you to carry out the behaviour that led to the emotion. If you feel good, you have the confidence to broaden your experiences; to reach out and connect with others and make a contribution to the world.

Feeling good enables you to think and behave in an entirely different way from emotions that make you feel bad. Emotions can be seen as an organising response, because they focus our thoughts and behaviour.

Emotions such as fear, anger, sadness, guilt and regret narrow your perspective. You focus on what's wrong, deal with the immediate threat. When, for example, you are faced with an exam, you might feel anxious. But this anxiety can focus your thoughts and behaviour and make it more likely that you will revise. Of course, the anxiety might be so overwhelming that you avoid the exam altogether. Your flight or fight response is activated and may cause you to, in the example of anxiety about the exam, withdraw or freeze. In another situation – one where you are angry, for example – you might attack or defend yourself.

Emotions such as jealousy, anger and disappointment contract your world, whereas emotions such as hope, compassion and happiness expand your world and the possibilities in it.

Emotions have a positive intent
Judging emotions as 'positive' or 'negative', 'good' or 'bad' isn't very helpful. In fact, as we've just seen, all emotions have

a positive purpose – to keep you safe, develop and maintain social ties and to develop our creativity and self-actualisation.

So, why do so many of us think that certain emotions are bad or wrong? It's all down to the beliefs and expectations that we grew up with. For many of us, instead of being allowed to experience and express our feelings, our emotions may have been ignored, derided, belittled or denied.

For example, if you were frightened of the dark and told an adult 'I want the light on, I'm scared', you may have been told: 'Don't be silly. Of course you're not scared.'

Or, perhaps you once said you hated your teacher, friend, sister or brother. The response? To be told you were 'wrong' to feel like that.

The problem is, though, that these sorts of responses did little to teach you about understanding and managing feelings and emotions. Instead, these responses established ideas, beliefs and expectations that certain emotions are 'bad' or 'wrong'.

At one end of the scale, some of us have learnt to be restrained: to deny, ignore or suppress emotions. On the other hand, some of us have grown up in families where it was quite OK to openly express emotions and feelings – an open expression of emotions was normal, with hugs and kisses alternating between tears and angry shouting.

The idea that we should aim to only have 'good' emotions, such as happiness and compassion, although well intentioned, is not helpful because it suggests that we should try to eliminate anger and jealousy and other painful emotions.

All emotions have a positive intent – emotions such as fear, anger, sadness, guilt and regret might not feel good, but they do have beneficial aspects.

As I've already explained, if you are faced with an exam, you might feel anxious. The anxiety might prompt you to avoid revising or not even turn up for the exam at all! But it has a positive intent – the anxiety can focus you and motivate you to revise.

What about a difficult emotion, such as regret? How can that be positive? The positive intent of regret is to prompt you to reflect and learn from what did or didn't happen so you can avoid making the same mistake in future. Regret is only negative when we are stuck going back over what did or didn't happen and becoming bitter or depressed about it. But it's not the emotion that is negative; it's your unhelpful ruminative thinking and the failure to learn from what did or didn't happen and move on.

Our beliefs about 'negative' emotions contribute to why our emotions sometimes feel overwhelming, and unmanageable.

But try to keep in mind that emotions serve a positive purpose. Emotions are communicating with us. They motivate us to take action in some way. Therefore, when you ignore, suppress or deny an emotion, it prevents you from understanding or connecting with the important information your emotions are trying to convey to you.

When you believe that it's wrong to experience and express feelings and emotions (your own or other people's), instead of managing them in an appropriate way you may find yourself dealing with emotions in inappropriate, unhelpful ways.

Maybe you deny or play down the fact that certain events or situations have happened – for example, telling yourself that you didn't really want the job you've just failed to get – to avoid admitting your disappointment. Or you tell yourself you're not jealous of your sister or brother who your parents appear to favour more than you.

But emotions want to make themselves known; they want you to be aware of them, feel them and act on them in an appropriate way. Denying, repressing and burying feelings does not get rid of them. Instead, when an emotion is buried, it leaks out in other ways: either in passive aggressive or aggressive behaviour. We look at this more closely in Chapter 5.

So, we've seen what emotions are, where they come from and why we have them. We've also seen that emotions have a positive intent. The next step is to understand specific emotions – their nature, levels of intensity, the differences, similarities and relationships between them.

Key points

- Emotions are complex reactions that engage our bodies and minds; they play an important role in how we think, feel and behave.
- Our emotions are generated by the amygdala; a small structure within the limbic system of our brains. The limbic system enables us to respond quickly, instinctively and without having to think. Another area of our brains – the neocortex – is the thinking, reasoning part.
- An example of the limbic system in action would be an occasion when you have a split second's awareness – an

inner voice – that tells you something in an instant. This is your intuition: an immediate knowledge.

- There are three main ways that emotions are useful: they help keep us safe, they help us establish and maintain connections with other people and they inspire our creativity.

- As well as enhancing and widening our experiences, emotions can focus or limit experience.

- Thinking of emotions as positive or negative, good or bad isn't helpful. Our beliefs about 'negative' emotions contribute to why our emotions sometimes feel overwhelming, 'wrong' and unmanageable.

- Although some emotions are painful, all emotions have a positive purpose. Emotions are communicating with us. They motivate us to take action in some way: to avoid danger and keep safe, and/or to develop and maintain our social relations and/or to develop our creativity and self-actualisation.

2
Identifying and Understanding Emotions

E motions, then, are a driving force; they play an important role in how we think, feel and behave.

It may be that there are just six basic emotions – fear, anger, sadness, disgust, surprise and joy – but there are many more emotions that we can experience. Below is a list of emotions. The list doesn't include every human emotion, it's just to give you an idea of the wide variety.

Adoration	Exasperation	Misery
Alarm	Excitement	Panic
Anger	Fear	Passion
Anticipation	Fondness	Pity
Anxiety	Frustration	Pride
Awe	Gratitude	Rage
Boredom	Grief	Regret
Compassion	Guilt	Resentment
Confusion	Happiness	Sadness
Contempt	Hate	Scared
Curiosity	Hope	Shame
Despair	Horror	Shock
Disappointment	Hostility	Shyness
Disgust	Humiliation	Sorrow
Dismay	Hysteria	Spite
Dread	Irritation	Surprise
Eagerness	Joy	Suspicion
Embarrassment	Loathing	Terror
Envy	Love	Vengefulness
		Worry

Emotional vocabulary

Which words do you usually use to describe how you're feeling? Look up those words in a dictionary or on a dictionary website. Do you agree with the definitions? Does the dictionary's definition of the word 'contempt', for example, reflect how you feel when *you* use that word? What about the definitions for 'happy' or 'sad' or 'guilty'? Does 'guilt' mean 'a feeling of responsibility or remorse for some offence or wrongdoing, whether real or imagined', or would you define guilt differently?

If, like many people, you are not particularly expressive when it comes to your feelings and emotions, you may not have a wide range of words you use to describe feelings.

What feelings words do you usually use? Can you find alternatives to those words? Are there any that indicate a subtle difference in meaning? For example, if you use the word 'angry' you will find that 'frustrated' and 'enraged' are similar. The obvious difference between these words is that they describe different levels of intensity of anger.

What about the word 'embarrassed'? Are there situations where the word 'humiliated' might be more appropriate? Could there be words that are closer to what you (or someone else) are actually feeling in some situations?

Although there are many emotions and many words to describe emotions, it's unlikely you use all the words available to you for describing emotions. Even if you do have a wide vocabulary for feelings words, you probably still experience situations for which there are, apparently, no feelings words.

> Look out for descriptions of feelings and emotions in novels, biographies and autobiographies. What words and phrases do writers use to convey particular emotions to you, the reader?

Can single words describe emotions?

Calliope Stephanides, the central character in Jeffrey Eugenides' Pulitzer-Prize-winning novel *Middlesex*, comments that 'Emotions, in my experience, aren't covered by single words. I don't believe in "sadness," "joy," or "regret" ... the language ... oversimplifies feeling. I'd like to have at my disposal complicated hybrid emotions, Germanic train-car constructions like, say, "the happiness that attends disaster." Or: "the disappointment of sleeping with one's fantasy." I'd like to show how "intimations of mortality brought on by aging family members" connects with "the hatred of mirrors that begins in middle age." I'd like to have a word for "the sadness inspired by failing restaurants" as well as for "the excitement of getting a room with a minibar." I've never had the right words to describe my life, and now that I've entered my story, I need them more than ever.'

Not only are there emotions that don't appear to have words to describe them, not all English words have equivalents in all other languages and vice versa.

In some cases, words do exist to describe those nameless emotions – they're just not English words. Which is a shame, because they often describe a feeling that is very familiar!

Here's a selection of some of those words:

- *Schadenfreude* (German) The pleasure derived from someone else's pain.
- *Gigil* (Filipino) The urge to pinch or squeeze something that is unbearably cute.
- *Litost* (Czech) A state of torment created by the sudden sight of one's own misery.
- *Pena ajena* (Mexican Spanish): The embarrassment you feel watching someone else's humiliation.
- *Fremdschämen* (German) Being embarrassed for someone who should be but isn't.
- *Meraki* (Greek) Doing something with soul, creativity or love; when you put 'something of yourself' into what you're doing. *Meraki* is often used to describe cooking or preparing a meal, but it can also mean arranging a room or choosing decorations.
- *Yoko meshi* (Japanese) *Meshi* means 'boiled rice' and *yoko* means 'horizontal', so combined, you get 'a meal eaten sideways'. This is how the Japanese define the unique stress induced by speaking a foreign language: '*yoko*' is a humorous reference to the fact that Japanese is normally written vertically, whereas most foreign languages are written horizontally.
- *Gezelligheid* (Dutch) The comfort and cosiness of being at home, with friends, with loved ones or general togetherness.

Are there any emotions you'd like single words for? I'd like a word for how I feel on realising I've forgotten about the tea I made for myself 20 minutes ago, that is now only lukewarm!

Emotional awareness: identifying emotions

Whether it's being turned down for a job or place on a course, hearing that a friend has just given birth or sitting in a traffic jam, these kinds of situations all have emotions attached to them.

A good way to start understanding your own emotions is to be more aware of the thoughts attached to them.

Try keeping a 'diary of emotions' for a few days.

Write down all the events, big and small, that happen over those few days. Events such as the long queue at the shop, cinema, bank or Post Office. The realisation you'd forgotten a friend's birthday. The meal in that noisy restaurant. The news from your brother that he's leaving his wife. A colleague's promotion. Finding something you thought you'd lost. Being asked to sponsor a friend taking part in a charity event. Again.

Once you've listed some of the events, identify the thoughts you had.

Although your mind may get busy when you experience emotions such as jealousy, anxiety and anger, for example, remember: emotions have a physical aspect too. So, your body can also clue you in to your emotions. When you experience a *strong* emotion, you really can feel it somewhere in your body – tight chest, stomach churning, racing heart, sweating and so on.

Sure, a sore elbow is a different feeling than fear; but who hasn't had a fluttering chest or stomach when feeling nervous before a job interview? So, as well as being more aware of your thoughts, start noticing the physical feelings that occur, too.

Below is an example of some events and the associated emotions – the thoughts, feelings and behaviour.

Triggering event	Possible emotions	Thought	Physical feeling	Behaviour
Transport delay	Frustration Irritation Disappointment Rage Anger	Not again. This is the third delay in two weeks	Tense muscles, clenched teeth – rapid breathing	Silently swore to myself but just sat there
Realisation I'd forgotten a friend's birthday	Mild panic Irritation Guilt	Shall I just send a text, phone her or send a belated card?	Stomach flipped over	Went out to buy a card
Finding my house and car keys	Joy Relief Remorse (because you'd blamed someone else for losing them!)	Thank God, I've avoided all that inconvenience	Stomach flipped over	Phoned partner to let them know

Deconstructing an emotion – disentangling what triggered the emotion from the thoughts, feelings and behaviour that occur – can help you to see it as 'just emotion' rather than getting caught up and overwhelmed by it. You unravel or disentangle the emotion before it unravels you!

The idea is not to obsess and overanalyse your thoughts and behaviour – just to notice the connections between events and emotions; thoughts, feelings and behaviour.

Taking time to deconstruct an emotion can also create the space and time you need to respond appropriately. When you are more aware of what you are experiencing, you can detach yourself from your automatic reactions and consciously choose your response to those emotions.

> Wisdom knows what feelings are present without being lost in them.
>
> Jack Kornfield. *The Wise Heart*

Learning to notice feelings and the type of events that trigger them can put you in a better position to manage emotions. Why? Because it can help you to identify unhelpful patterns of thinking and behaving, making it easier to understand what's going on in a situation and act accordingly.

Label the emotion

Labelling your emotion is also helpful. It means simply saying to yourself: 'This is an emotion. It feels like (for example) disappointment.'

OK, so you weren't happy that your colleague got the promotion, but was it anger, frustration or disappointment? Or was it something else? Reluctant to admit that it's jealousy, disappointment or contempt? Don't be. Emotions do not define you; remember, they are simply temporary internal messages to yourself that prompt you to act; to act in a positive way.

At this stage, you are not attempting to change anything about the emotion – just to be aware of it – the thoughts and feelings.

An 'open monitoring' meditation

A mindfulness practice, an 'open monitoring' meditation, can be helpful in becoming aware of your thoughts and feelings. Here's what to do:

- Simply focus your attention on breathing in and breathing out. There's no need to change your breathing; just breathe normally.
- When you notice that a thought has come into your mind, before you go back to focusing on your breathing, *acknowledge* the thought; tell yourself 'a thought has come into my mind', then return your attention back to your breathing.
- That's it. It's that simple.

So, for example, if you had a thought 'I must remember to phone my friend', you acknowledge that thought by saying to yourself: 'I've just had a thought that I need to remember to phone my friend.' And then return to focusing on breathing in and breathing out. Or, if you were feeling guilty about having been rude to someone else, you might acknowledge that by saying to yourself: 'I'm feeling guilty/regretful/ashamed.' Or whichever emotion you recognised yourself as having felt.

Practising an open monitoring meditation – it need only be for one minute each day – develops your ability to acknowledge your thoughts and feelings. It creates a space. That space can help you better respond to your thoughts and feelings instead of instantly reacting to them, getting overwhelmed or stuck in them.

Identifying emotions – other people's

Learning to identify and understand your own emotions is a good start to identifying and understanding other people's emotions.

It's not just what people say, but how and what they say that will allow you to better tune in to how other people are feeling. The chapter on communication – Chapter 4 – explores this idea.

Helping children identify their emotions
You can help children develop their emotional intelligence. Here's some suggestions:

- While reading stories to children, pause occasionally and ask the child to identify the characters' feelings in the story. Discuss how the pictures of the characters show their feelings. Ask questions like: 'Look at Jasper's face. How is he feeling?' 'How can you tell he is scared?' 'How do his face and body show he is feeling scared?'
    Help children identify the cues that suggest how another person is feeling. Point out facial expressions, body language, tone of voice and the context and situation. When you read out feelings words – puzzled, thrilled, impatient, worried, proud and so on – pull the appropriate face together.

- Play feelings games by asking children: 'Show me how your body and face would look if:
  1. you were given a present
  2. a big dog barked at you
  3. a friend put a worm in your hand
  4. you dropped your ice cream
  5. your friend fell over and hurt himself.'

    Change roles – get the child to think of situations and ask you to act out the emotion.

- Help children understand that people may have different feelings about the same situation: 'Alba is excited when there is a thunderstorm, but Oscar gets upset.' 'Kate likes to climb high on the climbing frame, but Jenny gets scared.' Discuss with them why they think that might be.

- Help children recognise that their feelings about a situation may change. 'Sanjiv, I think you're feeling sad now and want to be on your own? But later you may feel differently so do come and join the other children then.'

Cultural influences

Do we all experience emotions in the same way? No. Of course, people all over the world see emotions as pleasant or unpleasant, appropriate or inappropriate. But how, what and why each of us feel something, how we express our emotions and how we behave as a result, these things differ according to what is normal and acceptable in each of our cultures.

How does this happen?

In any culture, our emotions develop from basic emotions and automatic reactions to learned responses. For example, as babies we shriek with pleasure or howl with rage. But as we grow up, we are expected to learn to moderate these expressions of emotion.

The type of emotions – which emotions are 'good' or 'bad', where, when and how emotions can be expressed – is influenced by the beliefs and expectations of the specific community and society we live in.

For example, research by David Matsumoto, Professor of Psychology at San Francisco State University, showed that although in the United States it's acceptable to express emotions such as fear, anger and disgust when a person is in the presence of others, Japanese people only do so while alone.

In 2008, a further study by Matsumoto and colleagues found that, unlike people from individualistic cultures (cultures where the needs, wants, opinions and so on of the individual take priority over the group), individuals from collectivist cultures (cultures where the needs, wants, wishes and so on of the group take priority) were more likely to suppress their emotional reaction to any given situation. The reason being that it gives them the chance to evaluate which response is most appropriate in any one situation.

And, in another example, Professor Richard P. Bagozzi and his colleagues, in 2003, carried out a study on the emotion of shame. They investigated how shame – the knowledge you have done something dishonourable or inappropriate – is experienced and responded to by salespeople in Holland and the Philippines. In both cultures, shame is experienced in the same way – as a painful self-conscious emotion.

However, the study showed that there was a difference in how people behaved as a result of experiencing shame. For Dutch sales employees, an event that provoked shame was followed by a decrease in sales, poor communication and interpersonal skills. The employees interpreted the situation in a defensive way.

In contrast, shame experienced by Filipino sales employees created the opposite effect: better sales, communication and interpersonal skills. Shame resulted in the Filipino sales employees focusing their thinking and efforts on repairing and rebuilding relationships so as to increase sales.

So, for each of us, how, why and when we experience an emotion and how we behave as a result of any one particular emotion comes from a complex interplay of not just thoughts and physical feelings, but also social and cultural influences.

Emotions are complex

As we've seen, in order to understand emotions, we need to know quite a lot about them. As well as being influenced by culture, community and family – and as well as being made up of physical feelings, thoughts and behaviour – to make things more complicated, at any one moment it's possible to experience more than one emotion. Furthermore, one emotion could be contradicting the other! For example, you might be involved in an activity (rock climbing, rally driving) where you feel happy and scared at the same time. Or, attempting to finish a difficult task, you might feel both frustrated and hopeful.

Sometimes, certain feelings may also appear to 'hide' behind other feelings. For example, your four-year-old child lets go of your hand and runs out in the road. You snatch him back. You're angry with him. Your anger may, in fact, be mixed with fear; fear that your child could've been run over.

Or, perhaps your partner, son or daughter is late back home and you are unable to contact them. You're worried. And fearful. When they finally turn up (an hour or two late) telling you their phone wasn't switched on, your worry and fear might immediately turn to anger.

It could be that in these sorts of situations, you express a particular emotion because the underlying emotions are more difficult for you to deal with. In some situations, it's easier to express the anger rather than the fear, because expressing the fear makes you feel more vulnerable. And if you acknowledge that vulnerability, you've got a whole new set of problems to deal with!

Categorising emotions as a way to help us identify and understand them

Because our experiences are rarely straightforward, distinguishing one emotion from another is a lot like drawing lines in the sand in a desert. It can be hard to determine where one emotion ends or another begins.

When we consider two very different emotions – happiness or anger, for example – we know from experience that these emotions can vary in strength and intensity. But knowing how emotions can be categorised can further your understanding of emotions.

Psychologists and researchers have attempted to classify our emotions into different categories. Psychology Professor W. Gerrod Parrott agrees with Paul Ekman's theory that there are six basic emotions. But where Ekman suggests they are anger, disgust, happiness, sadness, fear and surprise, Parrot sees those six emotions as being love, joy, surprise, anger, sadness and fear.

Parrott has developed a theory to look at differences and similarities in the expression, meaning and response of emotions. He suggests that each basic emotion can give rise to secondary and tertiary emotions. So, for Parrott, there are six basic emotions, 25 secondary emotions and 134 tertiary emotions. For example, the primary emotion of sadness can give rise to a secondary emotion of disappointment. Disappointment can be related and give rise to the tertiary emotions of dismay and displeasure. And in another example, the primary emotion of joy can be related to the secondary emotion of optimism, which in turn can be related to hope and eagerness.

Primary emotions	Secondary emotions	Tertiary emotions
Love	Affection	Adoration, affection, love, fondness, liking, attraction, caring, tenderness, compassion, sentimentality
	Lust	Arousal, desire, lust, passion, infatuation
	Longing	Longing
Joy	Cheerfulness	Amusement, bliss, cheerfulness, gaiety, glee, jolliness, joviality, joy, delight, enjoyment, gladness, happiness, jubilation, elation, satisfaction, ecstasy, euphoria
	Zest	Enthusiasm, zeal, zest, excitement, thrill, exhilaration
	Contentment	Contentment, pleasure
	Pride	Pride, triumph
	Optimism	Eagerness, hope, optimism
	Enthralment	Enthralment, rapture
	Relief	Relief
Surprise	Surprise	Amazement, surprise, astonishment
Anger	Irritation	Aggravation, irritation, agitation, annoyance, grouchiness, grumpiness
	Exasperation	Exasperation, frustration
	Rage	Anger, rage, outrage, fury, wrath, hostility, ferocity, bitterness, hate, loathing, scorn, spite, vengefulness, dislike, resentment
	Disgust	Disgust, revulsion, contempt
	Envy	Envy, jealousy
	Torment	Torment
Sadness	Suffering	Agony, suffering, hurt, anguish
	Sadness	Depression, despair, hopelessness, gloom, glumness, sadness, unhappiness, grief, sorrow, woe, misery, melancholy
	Disappointment	Dismay, disappointment, displeasure

Primary emotions	Secondary emotions	Tertiary emotions
	Shame	Guilt, shame, regret, remorse
	Neglect	Alienation, isolation, neglect, loneliness, rejection, homesickness, defeat, dejection, insecurity, embarrassment, humiliation, insult
	Sympathy	Pity, sympathy
Fear	Horror	Alarm, shock, fear, fright, horror, terror, panic, hysteria, mortification
	Nervousness	Anxiety, nervousness, tenseness, uneasiness, apprehension, worry, distress, dread

Parrott's way of classifying emotions is useful to identify and understand the primary emotion that is the basis for the secondary or tertiary emotion. What do you think? Does the tracing back to the primary emotion explain anything about your or anyone else's behaviour, motivations or responses in a given situation?

Although both Parrott and Ekman suggest there are six basic emotions, Professor Robert Plutchik proposed that there are, in fact, eight basic emotions. He suggests they are grouped on a positive or negative basis; four of the emotions being the polar opposite of four others.

Basic emotion	Basic opposite
Joy	Sadness
Trust	Disgust
Fear	Anger
Surprise	Anticipation

For Plutchik, basic emotions can be modified to form complex emotions. For example, anger and disgust could combine to create contempt. Sadness and surprise suggest disapproval. Love is the combination of joy and trust.

Plutchik sees these eight basic emotions as being part of a 'wheel of emotions' because, he says, different emotions can blend into one another and create new emotions.

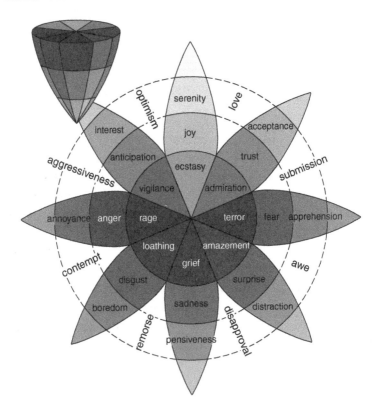

What do you think? Does the combination of, for example, annoyance and boredom suggest contempt to you?

In this chapter we've looked at identifying emotions. You'll have read that emotions are complex: influenced by culture, made up of physical feelings, thoughts and behaviour as well as having different levels of intensity. And, because of this complexity, recognising any one particular emotion in yourself or someone else is not always straightforward!

However, although there is no one definitive way of categorising emotions, thinking of emotions in terms of categories helps to provide a framework for us to understand emotions – to make sense and meaning of their nature, intensity, the differences, similarities and relationships between them.

And, like anything else in life, once you understand something, you're in a better position to manage it.

Key points

- Although we have a number of basic emotions – fear, anger, sadness, disgust, surprise and joy – there are of course, many more emotions that we can experience.
- Being more aware of your emotions (for example, by practising an open monitoring meditation) and the type of events and situations that trigger them can help you better understand and manage situations appropriately.
- Remember, emotions do not define you; they are simply temporary internal messages to yourself that prompt you to act in a positive way.
- How, why and when we experience an emotion and how we behave as a result of any one particular emotion comes from a complex interplay of not just thoughts and physical feelings, but also social and cultural influences.

- Although there is no one definitive way of categorising emotions, thinking of emotions in terms of categories helps to provide a framework for us to understand emotions; to make sense and meaning of their nature, intensity, the differences, similarities and relationships between them.

3
Managing Your Emotions

So far, we've seen that emotional intelligence starts with being *aware* of and *understanding* emotions; both your own and other people's. The next step is to develop your ability to *manage* emotions. Again, your own and other people's.

Managing emotions includes the following.

- Using your emotions to inform and guide your thinking and reasoning.
- Using emotions to help inform decisions about what to do and what not to do.
- Knowing when to respond immediately and when to step back, stop and think.
- Knowing how and when to express emotions in a way that is appropriate in any one situation.
- Being able to understand and manage other people's emotions.
- Knowing how to use emotions to build empathy and rapport with others.

Managing emotions doesn't mean controlling emotions. Controlling emotions involves attempts to dominate, suppress or restrain thoughts, feelings and behaviour. But when you manage emotions, the emphasis is on directing and influencing thoughts, feelings and behaviour.

When you try and control an emotion – avoid, suppress or deny an emotion (yours or someone else's) – you block the important message the emotion is trying to convey. And it can take a lot of energy to keep feelings suppressed. The effort can leave you stressed and exhausted.

Regularly blocking or suppressing emotions keeps you apart from others. The more you distance yourself from feelings, the more distant you become from other people – their emotions and needs. You can find it difficult to develop relationships and communicate effectively. Relationships and communication both depend on being in touch with your emotions.

> Each one of us makes his own weather, determines the colour of the skies in the emotional universe which he inhabits.
>
> Bishop Fulton J. Sheen

Take responsibility for your emotions

A friend losing something you've lent them, seeing your partner behave badly at a social occasion or being criticised because you made a mistake at work. How might you feel in any of those situations? Disappointed, embarrassed, upset? Hurt and angry?

A good start to managing your emotions is understanding that you create your own emotions.

People often say or think things like, 'She embarrassed me', or 'He makes me angry', or 'She made me jealous' or 'He's the only person that makes me happy'.

This way of thinking suggests that other people and circum-stances are responsible for your emotions. Not so. *You* create your emotions. And everyone else creates their own emotions.

If someone is upset with you for something you've done, you might feel shame or guilt. Shame and guilt are *your* reactions. The other person didn't make you feel guilt and shame.

Blaming someone else can be a way to justify how you feel. You convince yourself that you feel like this *because* of what the other person did. It's not your fault you feel this way – it's *their* fault. You don't like feeling like this, so you blame someone else. You take on the role of being a victim, convinced you are suffering through no fault of your own.

Own your emotions. Don't blame them on other people. Try to be aware of the times when you blame other people and situations for how you feel.

Taking responsibility for your emotions will help you to better manage them. Why? If you can take responsibility for your emotions, then like anything else that belongs to you, they are yours to manage; to influence and direct.

However, although you generate your emotions, certain things may trigger them. It's helpful to recognise and anticipate the 'triggers' that can set you off.

Know your emotional triggers

Someone on the train talking loudly on their phone, your young child refusing eating dinner, criticism from your parents, not getting the job, a colleague getting the promotion you thought you deserved more than they did, traffic delays and train cancellations.

Take a moment to think of and write down the sort of situations that you know will trigger difficult emotions. Ok, you can't predict every situation, but there are some that you know will push your buttons! What makes you scared? What winds you up? What sort of people and situations leave you feeling disappointed?

Very often, your emotions are triggered when your emotional needs are not met. Your emotional needs are what must be in place or what needs to happen for you to feel secure. Your unmet needs become emotional triggers.

Typically, your emotional needs include things such as:

- feeling safe and secure;
- feeling a sense of control and an ability to make choices;
- feeling a sense of belonging – friendship, fun, love and intimacy with significant people;
- feeling a sense of purpose; opportunities and the ability to achieve.

Children's behaviour is often an emotional trigger for parents. Vicky has two children aged six and eight. She explains: 'Both my boys are slow to get ready in the morning. I was constantly on at them to hurry up and get a move on. I'd tell them that they were making me cross, angry and stressed.

My badgering, however, didn't make them get ready any faster, and it caused a lot of stress for all of us. Eventually I changed my approach to dealing with the situation, and made them responsible for getting ready on time; I told them that if they were late it was not a problem – they would simply have to go and see the head when they arrived at school, and explain to her, then their teacher, why they were late. That did the trick!'

Learn to *respond* in a conscious, purposeful way, rather than reacting automatically. If you know the sort of thing that sets you off, you can develop strategies; strategies to manage difficult emotions and strategies to repeat enjoyable feelings.

Managing emotions, then, starts with identifying the emotion and what triggered it.

Stop and think

We've already seen that one of the prime purposes of emotions like disgust, surprise and fear is to keep us safe. If, for example, you are walking along the pavement and see a car careering out of control and coming straight for you, running out of the way is the wisest reaction.

However, emergencies aside, most situations need clear, calm thinking rather than blind, emotional reactions. In non-urgent situations, you need to be able to stop and think; to access the rational thinking part of your brain.

A good saying to remember is: 'Emotions say hurry. Wisdom says wait.'

If you can force the thinking part of your brain to work when you start to feel emotional, then you can overcome the rampaging emotional part.

This is the bit that so many of us struggle with. Over the years, you will have developed responses that become your default way of responding. They may be helpful or unhelpful responses.

But in situations where they have been unhelpful, how can you make a change? You need to slow everything down so that you can access the rational thinking part of your brain.

Just like a lever can be pulled that makes a train switch tracks so that it can go in a different direction, so you too need to change the course of your emotion.

You can do this by forcing yourself to:

- run through the alphabet backwards in your head;
- recall as many characters as you can in your favourite soap opera, film or novel;
- recall everything you had to eat yesterday – breakfast, lunch and dinner and anything in between;
- simply focus on your breathing – breathe in to the count of three and breathe out more slowly – to the count of five.

Whatever it is that you turn your attention to, make sure it's challenging enough to engage your brain but not so difficult that your mind jumps tracks back to your unhelpful thoughts.

Manage your emotions by looking ahead

You can also engage the thinking, reasoning part of your brain by looking ahead. Think about how you will see your reaction tomorrow, in a month's time or in a year's time. Will you be pleased? Your anxiety, jealousy, anger or disappointment, so real and important right now; where will they have gone in a month, a week or even a day?

Think to yourself: 'How will I feel tomorrow if I lose it and tell this person I have to see every day that they have a face like a smacked bum?' Maybe you won't regret it at all. But for the times when you do want to get a grip, try and look beyond the immediate and see the bigger picture.

Intense emotions blind us to the future and con us that now is *all* that matters. It can be helpful to keep in mind that you want to keep the job or a relationship with your sister, neighbour or colleague or whatever you are at risk of losing if you 'lose it'.

How can you remind yourself to stop and engage the thinking part of your brain? Wear a bracelet or another piece of jewellery that you touch or tug to remind you to stop and think. You could also write a note that says STOP! THINK! And place it on your computer, fridge or some place where you're likely to see it when you want to manage your emotions effectively.

Manage the physical feelings

Remember, emotions are made up of thoughts, actions and physical feelings. If you are experiencing an increased heart rate, quick, shallow breathing and muscle tension, you need to do something to slow down and manage those physical feelings.

For instance, anger and anxiety are often accompanied by faster, shallow breaths. So, a simple, effective way to manage the physical effects of anxiety and anger is through your breathing. Try this:

- Stop breathing for five seconds (to 'reset' your breath).
- Next, breathe in slowly for three seconds and then breathe out more slowly – for five seconds. Be aware that it's the out breath that will slow everything down.

This technique is probably not new to you – you may have heard it before. But the reason you will have heard it before is because it really *does* work.

It won't completely dispel the emotion – disappointment, anxiety or frustration – but it can dial it down a notch or two, just enough to keep you from saying, or doing, something you'd regret later.

Again, try it: it really does work!

Another way to manage the physical feelings and the adrenaline that's produced by strong emotions is to do something physically exerting. You could go for a run, a brisk walk or cycle. Do some housework – vacuum, clean the shower or bath. Do some gardening, sweep the paths or patio. If you're at work, walk up and down a few flights of stairs.

Again, you may have heard this advice before. But the reason you will have heard it before is because it really *does* work. These activities will all help to change your physical state and give you time to think – access the thinking part of your brain.

Music can influence how you feel. Let it all out; play loud, heavy rock or classical music and sing along with it. Or listen to slow, chilled music to bring those feelings down. The important thing is just to do or think something differently.

Of course, you might want to resort to your usual way of responding – consume yourself with whatever is making you disappointed, angry, jealous and so on. But if you want, or have, to change the situation, you can be your own source of distraction.

Remember, you can remind yourself to pause and manage the physical effects of an emotion by wearing an elastic band around your wrist, a bracelet or another piece of jewellery that you touch or tug to remind you to stop and think. You could also write a note that says STOP! THINK! and place it on your computer, fridge or someplace where you're likely to see it when you want to manage your emotions.

A range of strategies to manage your behaviour

Good emotional intelligence requires that we recognise and understand emotions and have effective strategies in place to be able to manage them.

How you manage emotions – yours and other people's – depends on, amongst other things, the context: the set of circumstances or facts that surround a particular event, situation and so on; the other person or people involved; your intentions and aims and the other person's aims and intentions.

Because managing emotions is dependent on so many variables, you'll need a flexible approach. Of course, if there was a standard response to every emotion and situation, you would always know how to act and behave; you'd know what to do and what to say.

But because each situation is different from another, you need to develop a range of strategies; a variety of techniques that you can draw on according to the circumstances.

Consider your options and take action

Often, difficult emotions are managed with a reaction that's simply a habit – a habitual way of reacting – whatever the situation is. Your emotions control you when you assume there's only *one* way to react. But you always have a choice, even though it often doesn't feel like it!

For example, if you're disappointed you didn't get the job offer or a place on a course, your reaction might be to phone up and demand to know why. Or it might be to email and politely ask for feedback. Or it might be to withdraw, drown your sorrows and tell yourself you didn't really want the job anyway. Whatever way you respond, you have a choice.

And, in another example, there could be someone at work who is sulking because you got a promotion and they didn't. You feel frustrated with that person. You could respond by confronting them and asking what their problem is. Or you could *choose* to ignore the other person's sulking.

Feed the other tiger

This story illustrates the concept of choice.

Once there lived an old man who kept many different kinds of animals. Two tigers that lived together in one cage particularly intrigued his grandson. The tigers had different temperaments: one was calm and self-controlled whilst the other was unpredictable, aggressive, violent and vicious.

'Do they ever fight, Grandfather?' asked the boy.

'Occasionally, yes they do,' admitted the old man.

'And which one wins?'

'*Well, that depends on which one I feed the most.*'

Being able to manage your emotions depends in part on how much you 'feed' a particular emotion. No matter what the emotion, there is always more than one way to respond. You could try the following:

- **Remove yourself.** If a situation and the accompanying emotion are overwhelming you, you may have the opportunity to remove yourself. For example, imagine you're on a train and someone's talking loudly on their phone. You're getting increasingly irritated. What to do? Remove yourself. Simply move to another train carriage. Supposing there might not be anywhere to sit in the next carriage? Take a chance – it's still a choice. You can choose to sit there getting more wound up or you take a chance and, at worst, end up standing. You choose.

- **Do something.** You could also ask the person to talk more quietly. Not sure how to do that without it becoming confrontational? This is a situation where knowing how to be assertive can be helpful. Read Chapter 5 to learn more about being assertive.
- **Don't do anything.** Unable to remove yourself or say something? You still have a choice. Because your behaviour is only one aspect of your emotion, you can choose to manage the situation by managing your thoughts or physical feelings in ways already covered in this chapter.

Reflecting on what happened

What do you do in a situation where your emotions did overwhelm you and prevented you from thinking straight and responding in a helpful way? Typically, you may now be feeling, guilty, embarrassed, annoyed or ashamed. Don't make things worse by allowing these emotions to paralyse you. Don't beat yourself up about it. You've already experienced a difficult situation and associated emotions. Don't add to your pain by getting stuck in shame, guilt, remorse and so on.

Instead, reflect on what went wrong. How could you change your response the next time in a similar situation? Just as you develop your cognitive intelligence by reflecting, for example, on where you went wrong with a maths sum or a puzzle, think how you could respond in a more appropriate, helpful way in a situation where you struggled with an emotion. That's being emotionally intelligent!

Talk about how you feel

Talk to someone. Even if it's your dog. Talking about things tends to help you sort out and clarify situations.

If you find you continually struggle with the same painful emotion or situation, talk with a counsellor, a support group or the Samaritans. Whoever it is, you may find talking to other people helps give you a different perspective. Be open to that different way of seeing things. Then you can decide how you want to respond.

Ask other people how they manage their emotions in particular circumstances. For example, ask: 'How do you keep so cool in that situation?' Or: 'Why doesn't that make you angry?' Or: 'How do you keep so upbeat after such a setback?'

Their answers could help to change your outlook, if you start to apply what you learn.

Managing other people's emotions

As you develop your ability to manage your own feelings and emotions, you'll also develop your ability to manage other people's.

You've probably been told before that you can't change other people; nagging, insisting, demanding or manipulating might work but it doesn't bode well for future interactions with someone. But what you *can* do is understand other people's motivations, needs and emotions. Once you have a better understanding of what someone is feeling – once you can make sense and meaning of their emotions – you are better placed to manage the other person and their emotions.

The chapters in Part 2 will help you further with this.

Key points

- Managing emotions doesn't mean controlling emotions. Controlling emotions involves dominating, suppressing or denying thoughts, feelings and behaviour. When you manage emotions, the emphasis is on directing and influencing thoughts, feelings and behaviour.
- If you try and control an emotion – avoid, suppress or deny an emotion (yours or someone else's) – you block the important message the emotion is trying to convey.
- Rather than blame people for 'making' you feel a particular way, taking responsibility for your emotions will help you better manage them. Because then, like anything else that belongs to you, they are yours to manage; to influence and direct.
- Once you've recognised your emotional triggers – the events that can set off strong emotional reactions in you – you can develop strategies to manage those difficult emotions appropriately.
- Emergencies aside, most situations need clear, calm thinking rather than blind, emotional reactions. So, you need to be able to stop and think; to access the rational thinking part of your brain.
- Your emotions control you when you assume there's only *one* way to react. But you always have a choice.
- In situations where you feel you didn't manage emotions effectively or appropriately, reflect on how you could respond differently next time a similar situation occurs.

- Talking to others about your feelings can help you clarify and better understand your feelings.
- As you develop your ability to manage your own feelings and emotions, you'll also develop your ability to understand and manage other people's.

In this chapter you will have read that taking responsibility for your emotions and knowing what might trigger them can help you to respond in a conscious, purposeful, appropriate way, rather than reacting in a random and uncontrollable way.

You will have learnt that you can identify and develop specific strategies – strategies that work for you, personally – to manage your emotions. However, emotional intelligence is not limited to specific strategies to manage specific emotions and situations. There is further scope for you to understand and manage emotions – yours and other people's.

In Part 2 we look at broader approaches to emotional intelligence: communication skills, assertiveness and positive thinking. You will learn that these attributes are an inherent part – a permanent and inseparable element – of emotional intelligence that can help underpin and support your emotional intelligence.

PART TWO

Managing Emotions

4
Managing Emotions with Better Communication

Managing other people's feelings and emotions

Just because you ask someone how they're feeling, doesn't mean that the answer you get will tell you how the other person is *really* feeling. What a person says about how they feel and what they *actually* feel can be two very different things. People are not always honest or clear about what they're feeling. They do, however, give clues. We all do. Through our nonverbal communication.

According to research carried out by Professor Albert Mehrabian, the communication of *emotions and feelings* is made up of 7% what is said, 38% tone of voice and 55% body language. This means that 93% of yours and other people's *emotions and feelings* are communicated nonverbally.

Nonverbal messages can create, for example, a sense of interest, trust and empathy between people or they can generate fear, irritation and/or disappointment. And, when they don't appear to match up with what a person is saying, nonverbal signals create a sense of confusion and distrust.

Nonverbal communication can *support* communication (shaking your head when you say 'no') or *emphasise* what you say and how you feel (thumping the table with your fist as you shout 'no'). Nonverbal communication can *contradict* a message you are trying to convey – for example, if you were to tell someone you like what they were wearing but 'pulled a face' to another person to admit that you don't really mean it.

Nonverbal communication can also *replace* speech to communicate attitudes, emotions and feelings. A thumbs up and/ or a smile, for example, to convey approval; or thumbs down and/or a frown to signal disapproval.

In fact, you can often understand how someone is feeling just by looking at their facial expression. The basic emotions – surprise, anger, joy, sadness, disgust and fear – are, it would seem, universal; not just in occurrence, but also with the facial expressions that appear on our faces whenever we experience those emotions.

Facial expressions allow us to communicate important things such as a potential threat to one another. Perhaps this is why some facial expressions are so universal.

Basic facial expressions – how they can be socially interpreted

Happiness. Happy expressions encourage others to approach and join in.

Sadness. A sad facial expression is interpreted to mean that the person has experienced a loss, discomfort, pain, helplessness. A sad face signals to others that this person needs comforting

Anger. Anger expressions serve as a warning to others – they convey hostility, opposition and potential attack.

Fear. Fear expressions communicate imminent danger, a nearby threat, a need to flee.

Disgust. Disgust expressions signal to others to stay away from something revolting and nauseating, such as rotting flesh, faecal matter or other offensive materials that are definitely not appropriate to be near or to eat.

Surprise. Expressions of surprise occur in response to events that are unanticipated, and they convey messages to others about something being unexpected, sudden, novel or amazing. Interestingly, the brief surprise expression is often followed by another facial expression that reveals emotion in response to the surprise feeling. For example, surprise to find your front door wide open, followed by anger when you realise you've been burgled. Or surprise followed by happiness when you bump into an old friend.

Although these basic expressions are automatic, they are also easy to put on and fake – to signal to others or to hide other emotions and deceive or manipulate other people.

Of course, it's not just facial expressions that can clue you in to how someone else is feeling. Other nonverbal communications can signal a range of attitudes and emotions too:

- Body language; gestures, posture, eye contact, the tilt of the head.
- Haptic communication; touch as a form of nonverbal communication – for example, a pat on the back, a grip on the arm can communicate clear intentions.
- Proxemics: the distance between people in different social situations.

(Continued)

77

Basic emotions appear to be easy to identify and understand. But others are harder to interpret. Why? Because, unlike interpreting basic emotions, with all other emotions, you can't rely on one single nonverbal signal – gesture, facial expression and so on – to tell you how someone else is feeling. It's important to know that you need to take into consideration a *combination* of nonverbal signals. You also need to take into account the context – the circumstances – of a particular situation.

For example, imagine you're a teacher and you ask a student if they understand something you just explained to them. They reply that yes, they did understand. The frown on their face could mean that they were feeling confused; that they did *not* understand. But that frown could also mean that they *did* understand and they were processing this new information to see how it fitted with what they already knew. It's also possible that the frown on their face was because they were in pain or had just encountered a bad smell!

However, if you then noticed that the student was frowning, slowly shaking their head, biting their nails *and* leaning over to look at another student's work, then that combination of nonverbal signs would lead you to conclude that, in fact, they did *not* understand!

Intuition

When it comes to understanding other people's feelings and emotions more accurately, you need to take a *combination* of nonverbal signals into consideration. It's this *combination* of nonverbal signals and the circumstances in which they occur that we rely on when we experience intuition; that keen and quick insight about someone or something that happens without any reasoning or thinking on our part.

Intuition is actually an unconscious process of tuning into and responding to a combination of nonverbal information in a specific context. (I mentioned this in Chapter 1.) For example, watch the clip of Barack Obama reaching out to a fainting pregnant woman during his 'Obamacare' speech in October 2013 (type 'Obama support fainting woman 2013' into a search engine). If you can, watch it before you read further.

You may realise that as you watched it, you scanned the whole scene – the woman and the people around her – to quickly pick up on what was happening there. You didn't stop to think and work it out, it just all became apparent.

In this example, context – the set of circumstances or facts that surround a particular situation – gave you clues about what was happening. The woman was pregnant, two people near to her looked concerned, you could assume she'd been standing for some time *and* it's likely she was in awe of the fact that she was standing next to the President of the United States. This combination of nonverbal signals and context in which the event occurred all add up in an instant to present a compelling message to you, the observer.

Combination of nonverbal signals

So, in order to better understand what another person is feeling, look for contextual cues – the bigger picture – and you will recognise how typical and appropriate a specific emotion is in a particular context. Look for the bigger picture as well as the details. Then, if you are in a situation where you don't believe what someone is saying, when it doesn't ring true or feel right, you will know it's because that particular combination of verbal, nonverbal and contextual cues doesn't add up.

Imagine, for example, that a colleague said that they were happy to meet with you to negotiate roles and responsibilities for a particular project. At that meeting, although they made eye contact and smiled, their body was turned away from you and their arms were firmly crossed throughout. You'll be aware that something isn't right – that it's likely that there's something about their role in the project that they're unhappy about.

Picking up these signs, you might challenge the other person; ask what the problem is. Or you might try a different approach in order to persuade the other person to be more receptive to your ideas and suggestions.

On the other hand, it might be that it's *you* that's feeling unsure and uncooperative. But, for some reason, you don't want to say so. However, you want to appear to be cooperative so you'll deliberately use facial expressions and gestures that give the impression that you *are* open and receptive to the other person's ideas and suggestions.

In fact, we've all used nonverbal communication to deliberately project feelings that we don't actually feel.

Whether or not this is acceptable depends on the situation. It's fine to create a confident manner – a balanced posture, calm voice and gestures – to help you look and feel confident for an interview or meeting or at a social situation, for example. You can read more about creating a confident attitude with your body language on page 87.

But in other situations, faking a gesture or facial expression can come across as phony and insincere. Why? Because the gestures and body language a person is *not* conscious of may give them away.

This is known as 'leakage' – an *unintentional* nonverbal signal. For example, although a person is all smiles and appears pleased that someone else won the award (*they* really wanted to win it), their lack of eye contact and limp handshake could be leaking their true sentiments when they offer their congratulations!

So, when you feel that someone isn't behaving with integrity, isn't coming across as honest or 'real', it's probably because their nonverbal communication doesn't match what they're saying.

Keep in mind that each person has their own individual body language called 'baseline behaviours'. These baseline behaviours are a person's usual way of acting and behaving. If you are aware of what is natural and typical for someone, you have something to compare against and you will be more aware when something doesn't quite add up.

Furthermore, there are sometimes subtle – and sometimes not so subtle – movements, gestures, facial expressions and even physical shifts in a person's body that indicate something is going on. Look out for changes; a change in a person's emotions will be evident in their nonverbal behaviour. Whatever is happening on the inside can be reflected on the outside.

Cultural differences

It is important to recognise that body language may vary between individuals, and between different cultures.

Cultural differences influence body language signals and their interpretation. For example, in some cultures, intermittent eye contact is used to convey interest and attention. In other cultures, although intense eye contact between people of the same gender is often a symbol of trust and sincerity, between opposite genders, anything more than brief eye contact is considered inappropriate. Additionally, in other cultures extended eye contact is considered a challenge.

In some cultures people are more likely to stand closer together, touch each other and talk loudly than in other cultures. In Japan, people smile frequently to express 'social appropriateness' rather than actual pleasure.

David Matsumoto, professor of psychology at San Francisco State University and CEO of Humintell, a consulting company that trains people to read human emotions, has found that there are culture-specific differences in tone of voice and vocal characteristics of people when they are lying. For example, his research shows that Chinese participants tend to speak in higher pitched voices when lying compared to truth telling; whereas Hispanics tend to speak in lower pitches when lying compared to truth telling.

Be aware, too, that as well as cultural differences, mental and physical difficulties can affect a person's nonverbal communication.

Develop your observational skills

Facial expressions, posture, touch and so on are all emotionally driven and can clue you into a person's true feelings and intentions at any one moment.

Developing your awareness of nonverbal communication and the combination of signals that people convey will make it more likely you will know when others are feeling, for example, disappointed, bored, irritated or pleased, more easily than if you just *listen* to what they say.

Practise 'reading' other people

- Watch debate programmes, interviews on the news and so on, and try to pinpoint the emotion underlying people's beliefs, expectations and opinions. Be aware of the nonverbal communication: the gestures, facial expressions, tone of voice and so on that are associated with that emotion. What *combination* of nonverbal language leads you to conclude that a person is expressing a particular emotion?
- Observe people on a bus, train, in a café and just notice how they act and react to each other. When you watch others, try to guess what they are saying or get a sense of what is going on between them.
- Be aware of 'matching and mirroring'. People who are in tune with each other 'mirror' each other; they tend to use the same posture and body language. At a social occasion you might notice that people who are getting on well together lift their glasses to drink at the same time. These are natural signs of a shared appreciation, harmony and understanding. Look for how other people do or don't

(Continued)

mirror each other. (It's interesting to note that singing and dancing are powerful ways that create connection because anything that involves moving or breathing in unison creates rapport.)

- Watch a drama or documentary on TV, turn the sound down and try to guess what emotions people are experiencing and displaying.

A word of warning: be careful not to get too caught up in analysing another person's nonverbal communication and don't always assume that you have correctly interpreted the meaning of another person's body language.

Managing your own emotions using nonverbal communication

Mostly, you are probably unaware how much you are conveying nonverbally. But as Professor Mehrabian's research shows; 93% of yours and other people's *emotions and feelings* are communicated nonverbally.

So, your nonverbal communication reveals your feelings and emotions more clearly than what you say.

The gestures you make, the way you stand or sit, how fast or how loud you talk, how close you stand, your facial expressions; they all send strong messages about how you're feeling.

Consciously or not, other people draw conclusions about your attitude and emotions; even if you're silent you are still communicating through your posture and facial expressions.

Your body language and nonverbal behaviour play a big part in whether the person you are interacting with is comfortable with you. And, when faced with mixed messages, either other people focus on your nonverbal messages or your mixed messages create confusion and distrust for the other person.

Being aware of what contributes to helpful nonverbal communication – body language, gestures and so on – will help develop confidence, trust and rapport between you and other people. This includes the following:

- Open body language and gestures. For example, arms by your side or hands loosely clasped. Try to use calm, flowing gestures rather than short, sharp movements which can distract or intimidate the other person.
- Facial expressions that reflect openness and interest, but which also respond to and reflect what the other person is conveying.
- An appropriate distance between you. Leave enough personal space between you and the other person so that they don't feel invaded, but you are close enough to feel comfortably connected.
- Avoiding fidgeting when listening or speaking. Habits such as pencil tapping or fiddling with jewellery may give the impression that you're distracted, nervous or impatient.
- Establishing eye contact. Whenever you greet a person, look into their eyes long enough to notice what colour they are. Then maintain appropriate eye contact. Don't stare the other person out, just show interest.
- Standing straight with your feet apart, your shoulders relaxed and your head held level makes you look sure of yourself. If you are sitting, you can look more confident by putting both feet flat on the floor, widening

your arms away from your body or placing your hands palm down in your lap or on the table. Stillness sends a message that you're calm and confident.

- Practise your handshake. The right handshake can give you immediate credibility and the wrong one can put other people off in an instant. So, no 'dead fish' or 'bone-crusher' grips, please.
- Smile. Smiling directly influences how other people respond to you. When you smile at someone, they usually smile back. And because facial expressions trigger corresponding feelings, the smile you get back actually changes that person's emotional state in a positive way.

The effects of posture on confidence

In a 2010 study by Professor Dana Carney and her colleagues, participants were asked to spend two minutes in one of two poses: either an open pose (leaning back in a chair, feet up on the desk, fingers laced behind the head, elbows out) or in a tight, closed pose (sitting with shoulders hunched, legs together, hands clasped in lap).

Interestingly, not only did the people who held expansive poses report feeling more confident than the others did, but they also experienced a measurable physiological difference: when measured, their testosterone increased by 19%, while their levels of the stress hormone cortisol fell by 25%. In contrast, those people who adopted the submissive poses showed a *decrease* in testosterone and an *increase* in cortisol.

So, you can influence how you feel by simply changing your posture. The good news is that there's no need to adopt a range of poses, gestures and expressions that feel strange or unnatural to you. You simply need to adopt one or two of the 'confident' gestures or expressions and the rest of your body and mind will match up.

Try this: confident body language

If you want to feel more capable and confident – not just *appear* confident, but genuinely *feel* confident – simply choose to do just one or two of these actions:

* stand or sit straight;
* keep your head level;
* relax your shoulders;
* spread your weight evenly on both legs;
* if sitting, keep your elbows on the arms of your chair (rather than tightly against your sides);
* make appropriate eye contact;
* lower the pitch of your voice;
* speak more slowly.

You can't control every aspect of your nonverbal communication; in fact the harder you try, the more unnatural you will appear. But if you can just use one or two of those things consistently, your thoughts, feelings and the rest of your behaviour will catch up.

It's a dynamic process where small changes in how you use your body can add up to a big change in how you feel, how you behave and the impact you have on other people.

Remember, emotions have three aspects: they are made up of thoughts, feelings and behaviour.

So, if you're feeling anxious before an interview or meeting a new group of people, if your thoughts are negative and you are experiencing physical feelings such as shallow breathing and a racing heart, it follows that if you change your behaviour, you can change those thoughts and physical feelings.

Which two nonverbal behaviours would you feel most comfortable using? Choose two and practise using them in a variety of situations. You don't need to worry about getting every aspect of your nonverbal behaviour 'right'. If you are being honest and sincere about what you're saying, the more likely it is that your nonverbal communication will reflect how you feel.

Verbal communication

Although nonverbal communication says a lot about a person's feelings and emotions, you can't always assume you've correctly understood the meaning of someone else's gestures, posture and expressions. You do need to talk and listen!

Often, when people talk with each other, they don't listen. You might be aware of what the other person is saying, but you may not be completely focused on the other person. You could be thinking about what you're going to say next – or you might be distracted by something else that's happening or you could be thinking about something else entirely.

However, there is a simple and effective technique to better ensure that you really are listening to the other person. And that is active listening. Active listening makes the other person feel encouraged to talk and understood. And active listening makes it more likely that you'll be able to understand what the other person has said and how they feel.

It is called 'active' listening because you are active in the process; you participate by consciously doing things to help the other person to express themselves.

Active listening

- Use nonverbal communication to acknowledge what the other person is saying. A simple nod of the head or an appropriate touch on the arm goes a long way to connect to the other person.
- Use 'minimal encouragers'. Minimal encouragers are small signals that let the other person know you *are* listening: words like 'uh-huh', 'yes', 'oh', 'mmm' and little actions like nodding in the appropriate places show that you are engaged in listening. They encourage the speaker to talk, with minimum interruption or influence by the listener. Be careful, though, not to overuse encouragers or use them in inappropriate places. This will give the impression of just pretending to be listening and is likely to discourage talking.
- Show whether or not you've understood. You can do this by summarising and paraphrasing what the other person has said. So, in your own words, express your understanding of what the other person has said. Typically, you would start by saying: 'Am I right in thinking that you said . . . ?' or 'So, you're saying . . . ?' Reflecting in this way gives the other person the opportunity to confirm that this *is* what they've said and how they feel. But, just as importantly, it allows the other person to refute or clarify what they've said. For example, you

might say: 'It sounds like you were upset about what happened.' The other person might clarify their thoughts and feelings and respond with: 'No, not upset, just let down and disappointed.'

Of course, it would be quite odd to repeat, or paraphrase, what you heard or tell someone what you think they might be feeling every time someone spoke to you!

The crucial thing is to listen *as if* you were going to reflect back. Whether you do so or not. This is why *active listening* – and in particular, listening as if you are going to repeat back what the other person is saying – is so powerful. It focuses your attention, helps you to listen, be aware of feelings and encourages further communication.

- Reflect feelings. Often, you can interpret the speaker's words in terms of feelings. So, instead of just repeating what happened, the active listener might add, for example: 'Sounds like you're feeling confused.' Or: 'You seem disappointed.'
- Name the emotions. Saying 'I understand' or 'I see' doesn't speak clearly or emphatically enough to the other person. Responses like: 'You seem quite proud of what you've achieved' or 'You look upset about the decision' demonstrate that you are trying to understand their experience and their perspective.
- Pick up on their nonverbal communication. Be aware of the connections between verbal and nonverbal communication. Do they all 'say' the same thing? Ask the other person – for example: 'Rachel, you look confused. Are you ok?'

In the context of emotional intelligence, active listening involves a focus on feelings – helping the other person identify and express their feelings. Just listening and reflecting on what you think the other person is feeling can have a powerful effect, without you having to do anything. For example: 'I can see that you are disappointed with the product and frustrated with the service you've received. Let me talk to my manager about what we can do and get back to you.'

You don't have to make the other person's situation your own, agree with the other person or let their feelings dominate yours. Your aim is to *understand* the person's emotions, not be overwhelmed or undermined by them.

You are simply showing empathy.

Empathy

Empathy is the natural ability that we all have to understand how and what someone else might be experiencing. When you are trying to be empathic, it means that you are willing to try and understand someone else's situation, their point of view, their thoughts and feelings. Even when they differ from your own.

Empathy is what makes you wince when, for example, you see someone stub their toe. You literally feel their pain. Empathy makes you cry at sad movies and feel angry when someone else suffers an injustice.

(In fact, some professions rely very much on a person's ability to empathise. For example, the most effective lawyers, doctors, politicians, nurses, teachers, funeral directors, DJs and debt collectors are all required to anticipate and understand the experiences and feelings of others.)

(*Continued*)

When you are being empathic, your aim is to *understand* the other person's emotions. So, for example, you might be with someone who is anxious about flying in an airplane. You are happy to fly; you're never anxious about it. How can you empathise? Because you *have* experienced anxiety about other things; driving a long distance on your own maybe, or job interviews, or giving a presentation or speech. So, your empathy comes from relating to and sympathising with the emotion – with feeling anxious.

Close similarities in background or experience can make it easy for you to assume you know what a person is feeling. You may have had the same objective experience, but empathy means understanding another person's *subjective* experience. For one person, for example, difficulty trying to put a five-year-old child to bed might be a drag. Someone else might feel that they're a failure as a parent. And, for one person, redundancy means an opportunity to do something new – for someone else, it might feel like they're on the scrapheap. So, in both examples, you are aiming to understand the associated emotions and relate to them.

One final important thing to note – emotional intelligence also tells you that sometimes you just *won't* get it; you won't be able to understand or relate to the other person's situation and feelings. But that's ok. You can still listen to what they say about it.

Successful emotional intelligence requires understanding that others' feelings and perspectives may differ from your own. Active listening makes this more likely because the emphasis is on encouraging the other person to express themselves and for you, the listener, to clarify your understanding.

Identify good listeners

Can you think of one or two people who are good listeners? How do they listen? How do they show they're interested and understand what other people say?

Asking questions

Observing and listening to the other person can, then, tell you a lot about how and what they think and feel. However, you might still not be clear about the other person's experience. There might well still be more to find out. You need to ask questions!

There are two types of questions: open questions and closed questions. Open questions usually begin with the words what, why, how, tell me, explain and describe. For example:

'How did you feel?', 'Can you tell me what happened?', 'What did you mean by . . . ?' 'Why do you think . . . ?'

Open questions can be asked if and when you need to clarify a point or find out more. Open questions give the other person the opportunity to say more. Conversely, closed questions, such as 'Are you OK?' and 'Do you know how to do it?' are usually answered with a single word: yes or no.

So, if you want to find out more about how someone feels and what they think, ask open questions: questions that invite explanations.

Don't be afraid to ask questions; don't think that the other person will think you weren't listening, or that you just don't understand. Remember, for some people – reporters, counsellors, interviewers, detectives and so on – asking questions is their job!

Your facial expressions, gestures and tone of voice all play a part in the answers you get when you ask questions, so be aware of your nonverbal communication. And be sure that your questions don't come across as interrogative, attacking, defensive or rude.

Ask questions in terms of feelings. Often, we ask questions in terms of thoughts and behaviour: 'What did you *do* about that?' and 'What do you *think* about that?' Do ask: 'And how do you *feel* about that?'

There is a difference in asking people how they feel over what they do and think. Remember, emotions are made up of both thoughts, behaviour and feelings. There are often times when it can help you and the other person if you simply ask questions about feelings.

Let the other person finish each point before you ask questions. Interrupting is a waste of time. It can distract and frustrate them.

Also, make sure that you give the person enough time to respond to your questions. Don't be afraid of silence. The other person may need to think before they answer, so don't see a pause as an opportunity for you to jump in with your thoughts and feelings. That means you're taking over with your own train of thought instead of being open to where the other person's thoughts are headed.

We all think and speak at different rates. If you are a quick thinker and fast talker, the onus is on you to relax your pace for the slower, more thoughtful communicator or for the person who has trouble understanding and expressing themselves.

Practise active listening

You can practise active listening with a friend. Here's how.

One of you talks for two minutes on one of these subjects, below. The other person must use active listening techniques to show interest and understanding.

When the speaker has finished speaking, the listener can reflect back on what he or she thinks the speaker said and how they felt – their emotions about the situation they were talking about.

- What you'd spend five million pounds on.
- The best and worst teacher you had at school.
- A time when you received poor service in a shop, restaurant or from a call centre.
- The best or worst job or holiday you ever had.
- What your ideal holiday would be.
- A pet you once had.

Talking to other people

Understanding and managing other people's feelings and emotions isn't just about listening to them and knowing the right questions to ask.

Situations like finding the right words to motivate others, knowing what to say when someone is disappointed, telling someone you don't want to do something and asking for support – all are helped by knowing what, when and how to say something in direct, honest and appropriate ways.

In the next chapter, we look at how assertive communication and behaviour can help.

Key points

- Research suggests that 93% of your own and other people's emotions and feelings are communicated nonverbally.
- You need to be aware of a *combination* of nonverbal signals – gesture, facial expression and so on – to tell you how someone else is feeling. You also need to consider the context – the circumstances – of a particular situation.
- Be aware, too, that cultural differences, physical and mental health and abilities also influence nonverbal communication and its interpretation.
- You can positively influence how you feel by adopting one or two 'confident' gestures or expressions. The rest of your body and mind will then match up.
- Active listening allows the other person to feel encouraged to talk and feel understood. And active listening makes it more likely that *you* will be able to understand what the other person has said and how they feel.
- The crucial thing is to listen *as if* you were going to reflect back. Whether you do so or not. It focuses your attention, helps you to listen, helps you be aware of feelings and encourages further communication.
- If you need to clarify a point or find out more, ask open questions. Open questions give the other person the opportunity to say more. On the other hand, closed questions, such as 'Are you OK?' and 'Do you know how to do it?' are usually answered with a single word: yes or no.

- Ask questions in terms of feelings. Often, we ask questions in terms of thoughts and behaviour: 'What did you *do* about that?' and 'What do you *think* about that?' Do ask: 'And how do you *feel* about that?'
- Be deliberate with your listening; reflect and ask appropriate questions. Remind yourself that your goal is to *understand* what the other person is saying, not to agree, disagree, be overwhelmed or take over. You are simply showing empathy.

5
Being Assertive

Assertiveness is an inherent part of being emotionally intelligent; assertiveness is a permanent and inseparable quality of emotional intelligence.

Both emotional intelligence and assertive communication involve identifying, understanding and managing your feelings. In clear, honest and appropriate ways.

Imagine, for example, that a colleague criticised a specific piece of work you had done, and she made unkind remarks about it. Not telling your colleague that you are offended by her remarks, because you don't want it to appear as though you are oversensitive, not only leaves you feeling upset with her but frustrated with yourself for not expressing your feelings.

You tell yourself that if your colleague had any respect for you, she wouldn't be so rude. As you ruminate on this, your resentment builds and you doubt yourself and your abilities, which lowers your confidence. This lessens your chances of asserting yourself. The result? You bury your hurt feelings for now, but they leak out in other ways; with passive aggressive behaviour, or at some point in the future you drag out other perceived injustices and provoke a row. That's neither assertive nor emotionally intelligent!

Assertiveness involves expressing your feelings, thoughts, opinions, needs and wants. When you are assertive you are able to stand up for yourself despite any fears and anxiety you might be feeling. You are able to assert your rights without ignoring the rights, feelings and beliefs of other people. In fact, when you are assertive you encourage others to be open and honest about their views and feelings. This helps create and develop empathy and mutual understanding. And that's emotionally intelligent.

Being assertive is one way to communicate and behave. To develop your emotional intelligence, it's helpful to be aware of other ways of behaving and communicating; aggressive, passive and passive aggressive. Each way of behaving and communicating comes with particular feelings attached to it and may be met with differing responses.

Aggressive behaviour

Aggressive behaviour and communication involve expressing your feelings, opinions and needs in a way that attempts to control other people and fails to consider their views, needs, wants or feelings.

Rather than being honest and direct, aggressive communication often involves being angry and critical. Typically, aggression from one person results in the other person responding in a nonassertive way. They might react aggressively: getting angry, snapping or shouting back. Maybe the other person will react in a passive way: with fear or anxiety and actually do or say nothing in return. Or a person on the receiving end of aggression might resort to passive aggressive behaviour: finding ways to undermine, sabotage or avoid you.

Passive behaviour

Another way of behaving and responding that is often unhelp-ful is passive behaviour. This involves *not* expressing how you feel and what you want. Instead, you submit to the demands, needs and feelings of others. When you are passive, you allow others to take responsibility, to lead and make decisions for you.

Others are often uncertain of your feelings, so are unsure how to respond to you; or they find it easy to disregard your feelings, ideas, needs and so on. Feelings of anxiety, helpless-ness and fear dominate.

Passive aggressive

Passive aggressive communication is an indirect and dishon-est expression of your feelings, needs and wants. Rather than state feelings clearly, you control situations and people in underhand ways; manipulating others into meeting your needs. Emotions such as resentment, contempt, jealousy and blame are dominant.

In a variety of situations, if you are passive aggressive, you blame others for 'making' you feel the way you do, when in fact, you brought about those feelings by your own actions and inaction.

You often suppress your anger and frustration and use a nonverbal way of expressing it; for example, giving others 'the silent treatment' or 'dirty looks' rather than letting them know what you are really feeling. You may also be in the habit of using sarcasm and other subtle ways to avoid con-frontation or avoid doing certain tasks.

When not being assertive is and is not ok

If being assertive is the emotionally intelligent way to behave and communicate, you might wonder why we behave in other ways.

There are a variety of occasions when it's an advantage to be able to behave in passive, aggressive or passive aggressive ways. For example, anger is a valid emotion. There is nothing wrong in being angry – it is how and when you express it that matters. There is also nothing wrong with being passive – keeping quiet and submitting to other people's needs and demands – when it's appropriate and as long as you don't always fail to speak up or speak out. There are also times when passive aggressive behaviour might be a preferable way to behave; to avoid a full-blown confrontation that might lead to violence, for example.

A demanding colleague, a waiter who ignores you, your hostile teenager or jealous sister; they are all capable of provoking a reaction.

But while reacting in an aggressive way might get you what you want in these situations, other people resent and dislike you; they fear and avoid you. Being passive – not being assertive with the colleague, waiter, teenager or sister – means you avoid conflict and those people like you and think you are easy to get on with. But they don't take your feelings and needs into consideration. You get taken advantage of, left out and have no control.

Passive aggressive behaviour is often useful to avoid head-on conflict and direct confrontation; you can manipulate a situation to get what you do or don't want *and* you don't have to take responsibility when things don't work out. (Clever!) But again, as with the demanding colleague, jealous sister and so on, other people get confused and frustrated by you; they may resent you and avoid you.

On the other hand, when you are assertive, you are aware of feelings, needs and wants – your own and other people's. Your needs are more likely to be met and others more likely to have respect for you. By taking other people's feelings into consideration, you build trust, rapport and respect. And that's emotionally intelligent.

When we are behaving and communicating in an assertive way, even if other people resent our determination and persistence, we are able to manage it.

That doesn't mean that assertive people never behave in an aggressive or passive way. But an assertive person will take responsibility for choosing to behave or communicate in an aggressive, passive or passive aggressive way. For example, if someone who is usually assertive is being aggressive, they will acknowledge it by saying, for example: 'Yes, I'm very angry.'

If an assertive person behaves in a passive aggressive way, they are aware of the need to achieve something without antagonising someone else; maybe even to avoid the possibility of violence.

If they respond in a passive way, an assertive person can admit 'I am choosing to go along with what other people want' or 'I am not going to offer an opinion' or 'I choose to withdraw'. They see it as the best option at the time, they know they've chosen to behave in this way, no one 'made' them; they take responsibility for submitting to others' needs, opinions or feelings.

In fact, assertiveness doesn't always mean being honest and frank – saying out loud exactly what you are thinking or feeling.

For example, we've all received an inappropriate gift from a well-meaning friend or relative and pretended to be pleased. Sometimes, being slightly less than in-your-face honest is the kind thing to do. Knowing when not to share a feeling or opinion with others is an important emotional intelligence skill, and relies on other qualities, too, such as sensitivity to others, empathy and respect.

What makes it difficult to be assertive?

Sometimes, though, even if you are usually quite assertive you may struggle to express your feelings, needs and wants. If, for example, you're worried about managing the other person's response – you think that they'll get upset, sulk, get angry or respond with indifference – it can be difficult to be assertive. If you feel unable to manage the consequences of saying what you think, feel or need, it can be difficult to be assertive.

If you're feeling tired or stressed, upset, anxious or angry, guilty or jealous, this can also stand in the way of expressing yourself assertively.

However, you can't expect people to read your mind; to recognise how you feel, what you need and want. If you want something, if something bothers you, you'll need to be assertive about it.

Do assertive people ever hesitate to say how they feel, what they do and don't want? Yes, they do. But they don't let feelings like anxiety and fear stop them; they think, take action and take responsibility for the outcome. They feel the fear and do it anyway!

Here's how.

How to be assertive: think before you say anything

Identify how you feel. Whether you want to ask someone to stop behaving in a particular way, are telling someone you don't want to do something or you want to explain *how* you want something done, these situations all have feelings attached to them.

So, start by noticing how you *feel* about the situation. Irritated or furious? Ignored and left out? Worried? Anxious? Remember, your feelings and emotions are internal messages to yourself that can help you understand what you do and don't want and can help you and the situation move forward.

Acknowledging how you feel about a particular situation can help you clarify what you do or don't want. For example, imagine that a colleague asks (for the second time this week) if you could take on some work that she doesn't have time for. Your feelings of irritation and resentment are telling you that you want to say no. But instead, you ignore your feelings and tell her to email you the details. How did that happen?

I'm not suggesting that you snap at your colleague and tell her where to stick it. No. Rather than let your feelings take over the situation, you let your feelings *inform* the situation.

What if you're not sure how you feel? Perhaps you need more information? How much work or how much time does your colleague need from you?

Still not sure? Simply say that you are not sure and need time to think about it.

There are a range of situations where either you're not clear about how you feel or your feelings are overwhelming you. Taking time to know how you feel about a particular situation can help you to decide what you do and don't want. Then you can respond in an assertive, emotionally intelligent way.

Imagine the builder, plumber or electrician you hired hasn't finished the work he or she agreed to do. How do you feel? Pleased? Thrilled? Of course not.

It's more likely that you're angry, frustrated or disappointed. The positive intent of anger and frustration is to motivate you to put right a wrongdoing. The positive purpose of disappointment is to slow everything down, give you time to accept what has happened, think about what you've learnt and can do next as a result of what has happened. So, think what the positive purpose of the emotion is – what is it prompting you to do?

Decide what you do and don't want. Having identified how you feel, the next step is to decide what exactly it is that you do or don't want to happen next.

Set limits for negotiating and compromising. Think about the extent (if at all) that you are prepared to negotiate and compromise. Your limits can also help you decide what you will do if the other person does not cooperate with you. What are you willing and unwilling to accept from the other person? You don't necessarily have to spell out your limits to others, but in a variety of situations, *you* need to know how far is too far. If you don't know what your limits are, how can you know if you're being flexible or just being pushed around?

Decide on consequences and solutions. Decide what the consequence or solution will be if you don't get what you want. We're not talking threats or punishments here. Threats increase the emotional temperature and make an argument more likely. Supposing the builder refuses to return and fix the problem. If you threaten them, you are warning them that something unpleasant will happen if you don't get what you want. If you think in terms of punishments, then you are planning to hurt them in some way for something they did or didn't do to you.

However, when you see things in terms of possible solutions and alternative ways forward, you are looking for a specific answer to a situation. When you think in terms of consequences, you are identifying a logical result. Solutions and consequences follow naturally from the other person's action or inaction. The first step of a consequence and solution to the builder's lack of cooperation, for example, might be to contact the Trading Standards Office for advice.

Take time to think of solutions and consequences, rather than give an emotional reaction. The most important question you need to ask yourself is: 'What do I want to accomplish here? A punishment or a solution?' If you have a Plan B – an alternative way forward – *before* you talk to the other person, you'll feel a lot more in control.

Think first! So, there are four steps you can take before you say anything. First, think how you feel about what you do or don't want or what someone else is asking of you. Next, decide what, ideally, you do or don't want to happen. Then think about your limits: the extent to which you're prepared to negotiate and compromise. Finally, identify a Plan B – an alternative solution or course of action.

How to be assertive: say it

Be clear and direct. Having thought about it, you now need to say what it is that you do or don't want. It's important to be clear and direct; no waffling or elaborate explanations! Using hints, excuses or sarcasm can distort or weaken the meaning of what you really mean.

So, simply say: 'No, I'm sorry, I can't do that. I have too much work of my own to complete.' Or: 'I'd like you to come back next week and finish the work.'

Acknowledge the other person's response – what they say and feel. Once you have said what you do or do not want, you *must* stop and listen to the other person's response.

Often, it's easy to go off course. Expectations and assumptions can distort what you think the other person has said. So, in these situations, before you reply, you may need to clarify what you think you heard the other person say. You don't have to agree with the other person's reply, just be sure that you have understood.

For example, to the colleague who has asked you if you could take on some of her work and it's not clear why: 'Are you saying you've just got behind, or that our manager has just dumped you with more work?' Or, to the builder: 'So, you're saying that you *have* checked the gutters?'

Restating what the other person has said gives them the opportunity to confirm or refute your understanding. How you restate what the other person said is crucial here. Say it with an enquiring tone, not a sarcastic one!

Accept the response but stand your ground. Calmly respond to the other person in a way that will both acknowledge you have understood what they've said, but also confirm that you are standing firm.

So, in our two examples here, your response might be: 'I know that our manager has dumped more work on you and you must be feeling stressed, but I have far too much of my own work to deal with.' To the builder: 'I understand that you think you fixed the gutters on the roof properly, but there's clearly something wrong and I'd like you to return and see what the problem is.'

Negotiate and cooperate. Being assertive does not mean that you will always get what you want. It means you can start from a position of stating clearly how you feel and what you do and don't want. It also allows other people to state what they feel or want and, of course, they might want a different outcome!

If they refuse to cooperate, resist the urge to back down, argue or sulk. Use your emotional intelligence: acknowledge the other person's perspective and feelings. Try to negotiate or compromise with him or her. Aim for solutions and alternative courses of action.

For example: 'How about we all get together and ask for a meeting with the manager and explain how we're *all* struggling with this extra work?'

And to the builder: 'Is there a day next week when you're in my area and you could just come and check it out?'

Try and offer an alternative that works for you and benefits the other person as well. That way, you've neither passively submitted to the other person nor been so dogmatic that they can accuse you of losing your cool and neatly side-step the problem – turning the focus on your inability to handle the issue.

Cooperation and negotiation allow each person to feel that their feelings and views have been considered and that any decisions or outcomes have come about through mutual understanding and negotiation. Remember, though, if you do negotiate or compromise, bend as far as you can but no further. Know what your limits are and stand your ground.

How to say what you do *not* want: the key points

- Notice how you feel.
- Ask for more information if you need it.
- If you don't want to do what the other person has asked, say no.
- Listen to and acknowledge the other person's response.
- Stand your ground and insist.

Or

- Compromise and negotiate.

How to say what you *do* want: the key points

- Identify how you feel and what, exactly, you want.
- Say what it is that you want.
- Listen to and acknowledge the other person's response.
- Stand your ground and stick to what you want.
- Decide what your next step will be if you don't get what you want.

Or

- Compromise and negotiate.

Other things to consider when being assertive

Start small. If the thought of saying what you want, what you think and feel makes you anxious, practise being assertive in low-stakes situations. Is everyone at work talking about how much they all love that new TV show? Don't be afraid to say that you weren't all that impressed. Speak up and say what you feel about it. Share your feelings. Get used to telling it how you see it.

With friends or family and planning a meal out? If you're keen to try a different restaurant, say so. Don't just automatically defer to someone else's suggestion. Chime in with where you'd like to go.

Once you feel comfortable in these low-risk situations, move on to other, bigger issues and situations.

Rehearse. Supposing you know that you are going to be in a situation – a meeting at work or a family get-together – where your ideas, opinions or feelings are often ignored. With a friend, rehearse the situation where you plan to assert yourself.

Or practise out loud, on your own. As well as thinking about what you're going to say, think about how you're going to *feel* when you say it.

Use confident body language. Remember, if you want to feel more capable and confident, simply choose to use one or two of these actions:

- stand or sit straight;
- keep your head level;
- relax your shoulders;
- spread your weight evenly on both legs;
- if sitting, keep your elbows on the arms of your chair (rather than tightly against your sides);
- make appropriate eye contact;
- lower the pitch of your voice;
- speak more slowly.

If you can just use one or two of those actions, consistently, your thoughts, feelings and the rest of your behaviour will catch up. It's a dynamic process where small changes in how you use your body can add up to a big change in how you feel, how you behave and the impact you have on other people.

Be aware of 'paraverbal' communication: how you say something. Be aware that the tone, pitch, volume, rhythm, inflexion and the speed that you speak all provide subtle but strong clues to your true feelings and intentions.

Standing your ground. If you stand your ground, take responsibility for the outcome. Sure, there may be consequences for the other person if they don't do what you want. But there may also be consequences for you when you don't do what *they* want. The other person might sulk, get angry or burst into tears. They may stop talking to you or tell everyone what an awful person you are. If you stand your ground, you must accept that there may be consequences.

Say no without lots of excuses and apologies

You only need one genuine reason for saying no. Just politely say what you need to say and wait to see how the other person responds.

Say: 'I can't help you with your work. I've got too much of my own to do.' Rather than: 'I would help you but I've got too much of my own work and I've got a headache and I've got to go out and buy some lunch – I forgot to make sandwiches this morning.'

If you give too many excuses, the meaning and value of your response starts to look weak and dishonest. It also gives the other person the opportunity to undermine your excuses. For example, they might reply with: 'Hey, I've brought plenty of lunch with me – I'll share it with you then you'll have a spare half hour to help me.'

Try getting out of that!

All you need is one valid reason why you do or do not want to do something. Remember, acknowledge the other person's situation, but stand your ground. 'I know you are disappointed, but I have too much of my own work to do.'

Stay calm. If someone disagrees or disapproves of your choice, opinion or feelings, don't get angry or defensive. Either acknowledge what they've said and restate your opinion, or disengage yourself from the situation and the other person. It's particularly important, if your own or someone else's safety is at risk, to disengage in as calm and nondismissive a way as possible.

If you find yourself responding emotionally to what someone said, say so. Remember to own your feelings. You might say: 'You appear to be saying/feeling . . . and now I'm feeling . . .'.

Remember: you don't have to be assertive – it's a choice

A common mistake many people make on the path to being more assertive is to try to be assertive all the time, in every situation. Remember, assertiveness depends on the context, situation and the other people involved.

Sometimes a more aggressive approach *might* be more appropriate. Other times, it might be more appropriate to be passive and submit to others' needs. Whether it's doing the dishes, mowing the lawn or helping someone else out with their work – even though you've acknowledged to yourself how you feel (reluctant), there are times when you do need to suck up your feelings and just do it. With good grace!

You might think that in situations where you choose to submit or withdraw from a situation, you are being weak and powerless, or that you will lose the respect of others. Not so! As long as you accept responsibility for your actions and don't blame the other person for 'making' you do something, you are demonstrating your level of security.

How do you know when you should or shouldn't assert yourself?

Here are a few questions to consider before choosing to be assertive.

- How much does it matter to you?
- Will you regret it if you are not assertive in this situation?
- Are you looking for a specific outcome or just to express yourself?
- What are the probable risks and consequences of your possible assertion?
- Might asserting yourself make things worse?

Remember, being assertive means saying what you do and don't want, clearly and honestly, and at the same time taking into consideration the other person's feelings, needs and wants. That's emotionally intelligent!

Key points

- Being assertive is one way to communicate and behave. There are other ways: aggressive, passive and passive aggressive behaviour and communication. Each way has its advantages and disadvantages.
- An assertive person takes responsibility for how they behave or communicate; they don't blame others for 'making' them respond in a particular way.
- Even if you are usually quite assertive, it's not always easy; if you're stressed or upset or if you're concerned about the other person's response, for example.
- To know when you should or shouldn't assert yourself in any one situation, ask yourself questions such as: 'How much does it matter to me?' 'Will I regret it if I'm not assertive?'

- Want to assert yourself but still feeling reluctant to say what you feel, what you do or don't want? Have courage: feel the fear and do it anyway!
- There are four steps you should take before you say anything. First, think how you feel about what you do or don't want, or what someone else is asking of you. Next, decide what, ideally, you do or don't want to happen. Then think about your limits: the extent to which you're prepared to negotiate and compromise. Finally, identify a Plan B: an alternative solution or course of action.
- Other things to consider when being assertive are the following:
  - Start small; practise being assertive in low-stakes situations.
  - Use confident body language.
  - Be aware of *how* you say something.
  - Say no without lots of excuses and apologies; you only need one genuine reason for saying no.
  - Know that if you stand your ground, you must accept that there may be consequences.
  - Stay calm. Disengage if there's a risk to your own or someone else's safety.
- Remember: you don't have to be assertive in every situation; it's a choice.

6
Positive Thinking

We don't see things as they are, we see them as we are.

Anaïs Nin

Imagine you have a drink in front of you – a glass of water or orange juice, beer or wine. You've drunk half of it when the phone rings and you wander off into another room as you talk to the other person. When you return to the room, you remember your drink.

Is your glass half empty or half full?

You have probably heard that question before. This idiom is often used to explain how people perceive events. We each have our own interpretation of reality; some of us may be more inclined to see particular situations or life in general in a positive way. Others interpret events in a more negative light.

Do you see you your glass as being half full? Could be you're an optimist. Glass half empty? Maybe your worldview is more pessimistic.

The positive thinking that typically comes with optimism is a key part of emotional intelligence. Why? Because emotional intelligence involves managing emotions in a positive, optimistic way; with a positive mindset.

Having a positive outlook does not mean denying the difficult emotions or ignoring the challenging aspects of life. Positive thinking means that you approach the difficulties in a more positive and productive way.

You acknowledge – recognise the existence of – feelings such as jealousy, disappointment, guilt, anxiety and so on, but rather than let them drag you down into a spiral of negative thinking, you know that these emotions have positive intentions. You acknowledge – not deny, ignore or avoid – the difficulties and respond accordingly. Having acknowledged the negative aspects, you focus on the good things in a situation, try to see the best in other people, and view yourself, your emotions and your abilities in a positive light.

> Positive thinking is not just the feeling you have when good things are happening in your life – when it's easy to feel optimistic. It is about being able to maintain that feeling of hopefulness and motivation, whatever is happening.
>
> Sue Hadfield

Self-talk

Becoming more positive often starts with being more aware of your self-talk. Self-talk is the endless stream of thoughts that run through your head every day, rather like the moving text at the bottom of a 24-hour news channel.

Self-talk may be neutral: 'I think I'll decorate the kitchen.' It can be positive, encouraging and empowering: 'I could ask for some help with this and I'm sure I'll be able to do it.' Or negative: 'It's going to be a struggle – I'll do it all wrong, I'll bet.'

If the thoughts that run through your head are mostly negative, you see problems and difficulties. If your thoughts are positive, you're likely to see options and possibilities in a situation and expect the most favourable outcome.

The way we think – whether you are more inclined to be a negative or a positive thinker – is related to what psychologist Professor Martin Seligman says is our 'explanatory style'. Our explanatory style helps us make sense of the events and experiences in our lives.

When an event occurs, Seligman suggests that if you have an optimistic explanatory style you will tend to think that the effect will be long lasting and will positively affect other situations. Rather than spending a lot of time berating yourself or passing the blame when things go wrong, if you have a positive explanatory style, you simply acknowledge that something didn't turn out as well as was hoped and look to see what you can do to make things right. You also tend to see difficulties and challenges as unusual and temporary; only affecting the present situation.

When you are optimistic and have a positive explanatory style, it allows you to feel in control of a situation and believe there is something you can do to manage it and the accompanying feelings; your own and other people's. You have a tendency to put the most favourable construction upon actions and events and anticipate the best possible outcome.

In contrast, negative thinking and a negative explanatory style involves focusing only on the difficult, undesirable aspects of a situation.

For example, imagine that you have got to the end of a busy day at work. You gave a presentation and completed a report ahead of time, but you forgot to return an important phone call. Despite the successes of the day, that evening you find yourself ruminating on that one oversight, telling yourself that you're hopeless. You worry about what your manager will say. Instead of acknowledging the positive aspects of the day and deciding what positive actions you can take tomorrow about the one mistake, you focus and get caught up with the one negative aspect.

Seligman suggests that as a result of the negative outcome of past experiences, negative thinkers have *learned* to become hopeless and resigned. He calls it 'learned helplessness'. It happens over time as you experience the world around you, including how you were raised, educated and treated through life. If the messages you have received from others are negative, you learn to believe (rightly or wrongly) that you have little or no control over current and future events. And, not surprisingly, memories of previous experiences influence how you respond emotionally to situations.

Viewing mistakes, difficulties and disappointments as inevitable and persistent and difficult to bounce back from can have a detrimental impact on your state of mind.

You can, however, learn to think in a more positive way. It *is* possible to overcome negative thinking by learning new explanatory styles. If you consciously change your self-talk, you can change how you think about yourself and the world. And, if you change the way you see yourself and the world, you'll find that difficult and painful emotions make fewer appearances and/or are less of a struggle to deal with.

How to become a positive thinker

Live your life as if everything is rigged in your favour.
Arianna Huffington

Certainly, there are times when narrowed, negative thinking – thinking about the worse that can happen – is actually a good thing; in some situations, negative thinking can actually lead to positive outcomes. If, for example, you are worried about passing a test, an exam or an interview, fearing the worst – thinking you are going to fail – should motivate you to prepare well so that the worst is less likely to happen.

And, in other situations, feelings of sadness and disappointment over not getting the job you hoped for slow you down and focus your attention on your loss so that you can adjust to it.

Challenging, difficult things happen in life and you'll feel negative. That's normal. A negative outlook only becomes a problem when you become stuck in that way of thinking – when it becomes your default way of thinking.

Being positive and optimistic involves an open mind, making it a crucial element of improving your emotional intelligence. You can learn to have a more positive mindset. Here's how.

The first step is to be *aware* of your self-talk – that inner voice that directs your thinking and shapes your emotions, your beliefs and your actions. It is so easy to fall into the trap of negative thinking. More often than not, you will not even notice you are doing it.

Try this: write a thought diary

One way to become aware of your thoughts is to write them down. Write a thought diary for a few days. With each difficult or stressful event or experience – losing something, a cancelled train, being unable to find a parking space, the printer running out of ink, a problem with a family member, for example – write down the associated thoughts and feelings that occurred. Do this for a week or more and you can begin to identify your own 'explanatory style'.

The next step is to highlight all the negative thinking and then write out alternative, more positive ways of thinking. For example, 'Oh no, I forget to make that important phone call' could be changed to 'I can send an email now to apologise for not phoning and suggest a time that I could call tomorrow'.

When the negative thoughts occur, ask yourself: 'How does it help me to think negatively like this?' And: 'Is this situation as bad as I'm making it out to be?' It's ok to have negative thoughts – what's not good is to stay stuck in those thoughts.

Reflect on what you think about situations and how your thoughts make you feel and behave. Be aware of how long you stay stuck in negativity. The more you are aware, the more likely it is that you will avoid falling into thinking traps.

Practise being aware of negative thinking by noticing other people's 'explanatory style'. People you live and work with, characters in novels, TV dramas and films; what are their comments – what do you hear them say about the events that happen in their lives?

An experience of keeping a thought diary

Elana kept a thought diary for a week.

'I wrote down both the small and big events that happened each day, things like being stuck in a traffic jam for half an hour, on my way to a meeting, the hairdresser cancelling my appointment, finishing a report I had to write, listening to my sister complain about her partner, going to see a film that turned out to be rubbish, getting a promotion, planning next year's holiday.

It was interesting to notice the emotions attached to my thoughts. For example, when I finished the report, I was pleased; but a short while later, I began to feel unsure and concerned that my manager might not like it.

Keeping a track of my thoughts helped me identify the emotions attached to my thinking, to understand how I see myself and others.'

Event	Thought	Positive thought
Stuck in a traffic jam.	Typical. This always happens to me.	Thankfully, I can listen to the radio to take my mind off it.
Planning next year's holiday.	It's always left to me to organise the holiday.	I'm going to ask my partner to organise one aspect of it – I could ask him to sort out the car hire.
Watching a film that turned out to be rubbish.	What a waste of time and money that was.	The last four films I went to see were good. One bad one out of five isn't so terrible.

Once you're more aware of the self-talk that directs your thinking and shapes your emotions and responses, you can choose whether to dwell on negative, unhelpful thoughts or replace them with positive, encouraging and empowering thoughts.

Try this: think positive!

Aiming for a positive outlook means replacing the unhelpful thinking patterns with thoughts that actually help you. Take small steps. Identify a single specific event in your life that occurs on a daily basis – your journey to work, interacting with colleagues or clients or a family member, doing housework – where you could change the way you think.

Certainly it takes conscious effort to be aware of and replace negative thoughts. Here's two ways to remind yourself to do so.

- Stick a note on your fridge or computer that asks: 'WHAT ARE YOU THINKING?'
- Wear an elastic band round your wrist – each time your mind starts thinking in a negative way, snap the band. A useful short, sharp reminder to change your thinking!

It's about taking a proactive approach to your life. Instead of feeling hopeless or overwhelmed, positive thinking allows you to identify feelings and emotions and manage them by letting them inform you in more positive ways.

Beliefs and thoughts

Your beliefs and the strength of your beliefs are the source of power behind your emotions. Change what you believe or expect and you can change the emotion. When you change your beliefs, you change your emotional reaction to an event or experience.

Rational-emotive psychologist Albert Ellis talked about the 'A-B-C' model of emotion:

- A: Activating event. For example, a friend turns down your invitation to go out for dinner together.
- +B: Belief. You therefore believe that no one likes you.
- =C: Consequence. You feel frustrated and rejected.

To change the consequence – your emotion – you need to change your beliefs.

Of course, you could choose to spend a long time examining your thoughts: 'Why do I think like this? Where did that way of thinking come from? Whose fault is it?' and so on. Or you could just focus on *changing* your thoughts and beliefs; choosing to focus on the more positive way of thinking. This, by the way, is the principle behind cognitive behavioural therapy (CBT). CBT focuses not on what happens to us, but on how we think about what happens to us and how we behave as a result of the way we think. CBT looks at whether our thinking and behaviours are helping our situation or keeping us stuck, or even making things worse. And, if our thinking and behaviours are not helpful, CBT looks at how we can best change what we think and do.

So, in the above example, rather than believe that a friend turning down your invitation to go out for dinner together is evidence that no one likes you, you can instead change your perspective and choose to believe a more positive reason – maybe that, as they explained to you, because of their work and caring responsibilities, they really are too exhausted at the end of the day to go out in the evening.

Train your brain to think positively

Changing negative thought cycles is a process that takes time. You can, though, train your brain to think more positively.

You simply need to give your brain lots of opportunities to think more positively. The idea here is that, like anything else that is practised and constantly repeated, the new behaviour or way of thinking soon becomes automatic: it becomes a habit. A positive habit.

There's a scientific explanation for this: the core components of the brain are neurons – cells that process and transmit information in your brain. The interconnections between neurons mean that, when you do something new, you create new connections, or pathways, between those neurons.

If you change how you think or what you do, then new pathways are formed. If you continue using these new pathways, they become much stronger. Eventually, they will replace the old ways of thinking and behaving; the old ways – or paths – will weaken and fade.

So, when it comes to positive thinking, if you can replace negative thoughts with positive ones, you will create new, different neural pathways; positive pathways for thinking about yourself, other people and events.

Try this: practise positive thinking

To train your brain to think more positively and strengthen this element of your emotional intelligence, try out some of the following:

Cultivate an open mind. Openness and positivity go hand in hand when it comes to emotional intelligence. Be open to different ideas and opinions so that you are in a position to consider new possibilities in a positive manner. This will also help develop your empathy: your ability to see things from another person's perspective.

One way you can strengthen this element of your emotional intelligence is to listen to debates on television or the radio. Programmes like BBC 1's Question Time, BBC 2's Newsnight, Channel 4's News and Radio 2's Jeremy Vine Show seek to present more than one view. Watch and listen to these programmes and identify the different viewpoints. See how the same issue can be regarded in different ways.

Imagine positive outcomes. It's not just positive self-talk that can make a difference; what you 'see' can also help you to think in a more positive, optimistic way. Fear, worry and doubt can create negative images – obstacles and difficulties – in your mind.

If what you can 'see' are obstacles, then you have created images that will block you. On the other hand, emotions such as courage, determination and resolve create positive images that allow you to manage yourself more effectively.

For example, supposing you have to drive somewhere you have never been to before. If you visualise yourself getting lost on that journey, you are accessing negative neural pathways. If, instead, you visualise yourself coping – leaving in plenty of time, using a sat nav or map and asking for directions if you do get lost – you are accessing the positive neural pathways and you feel more inclined to believe that you will be able to manage.

Visualisation is important because seeing yourself coping makes your brain believe that it is indeed possible. Start

(Continued)

to change your old, internal disempowering pictures to images of something that you wish to experience.

Remember when you've done well. Identify and even write down situations where you have experienced difficult events or emotions and feelings but managed them successfully. For example, you made amends when you felt guilty about letting someone else down. Remind yourself of these times as a way of helping you access positive thoughts and images.

It makes sense really, doesn't it? You already know that recalling a negative memory can put you in a bad mood. So, focus on thinking about happy memories.

Three good things. When you turn your thoughts to the good things in your life, you are using those positive neural pathways; you're thinking positively!

On a day where not much seems to have gone right, instead of focusing on the negative events, start a new habit: identify and reflect on the small pleasures – things that made you feel good. The smallest things can make a difference. However small and seemingly insignificant, gratitude simply requires you to notice the small pleasures around you.

Here's a simple but effective technique for raising your gratitude levels and developing your sense of optimism: before you go to bed each night, perhaps when you're brushing your teeth, identify three good things that have happened during the day. You may want to write them down, or you may simply reflect on what those things are. Appreciate just knowing that you had good in your day so that, whatever the other difficulties, you did in fact have things that made it all worthwhile. If you can find a way to remind yourself to do this every day for a couple of weeks, you will soon find yourself actively looking for things to appreciate and it will become a habit.

So yes, you missed the bus, for example; but you then had a spare 15 minutes and you found the perfect birthday present for your Mum in a nearby shop *and* you didn't have to stand in the rain.

What else was good? Perhaps you noticed that the daffodils had started blooming in your garden? *And* someone else loaded the dishwasher that evening.

Look for what's good. Find the good in events, people and things around you, all of the time. Find at least one thing you like about every person you meet and every place you go.

Use a 'beginner's mind'. Does someone or something annoy you? Try seeing those people or events in a new light. You can do this with a 'beginner's mind'. Beginner's mind is a concept from mindfulness. It means that rather than respond to other people and events in the same old ways – ways from the past – you put aside your beliefs and the conclusions you came to previously and you open yourself to new possibilities. Approach each person or event in the present, as if for the first time – with an open, positive mind.

Be nice. Positivity attracts positivity in the same way that negativity attracts negativity. If you are kind, nice and helpful to people, you can expect the same treatment back. When you are consciously aware of others' needs, opportunities to help will make themselves known. Phone someone you know who would enjoy a chat; hold the door open for others; make brief eye contact and smile; bake someone a cake; offer to help someone with their gardening or decorating.

Identify positive people in your life and spend more time with them. Optimism is infectious. Misery is also infectious. Which would you prefer? If you want to 'catch' optimism, spend time with people who make you feel good: people who make you laugh, are supportive and kind.

(Continued)

Show appreciation. Thank those in your life who make it better and happier. Again, making yourself think about the good in other people forces you to access those positive neural pathways.

Make time for laughter. Go to a comedy club or watch a comedy on screen. Stand up comics usually have routines that encourage you to see things differently. Spend time with friends who make you laugh.

Read. Read about people who have fought fear with courage and have succeeded in life, from explorers to entrepreneurs. Through reading, you will gain new knowledge and understanding and you will see that you're not alone in your effort to focus on the positive aspects of life.

Making some of these ideas a habit is what reinforces the neural pathways that can really help to establish a positive mindset. It's far easier to get out of a negative state of mind when you know what works for you – what kinds of things can help you access positive ways of thinking. So do try some or all of these suggestions for developing a positive mindset. See which ones work for you – and repeat often!

Flow activities

It's helpful to seek out activities that provide you with a sense of contentment and satisfaction. But when your mind is preoccupied with negative thoughts, is there a way to divert your mind for long periods, without too much effort? Yes, there is. It's called 'flow'.

Have ever started a task or activity and become so absorbed in what you were doing that time passed without you noticing? If so, then you achieved that state of mind known as 'flow'.

You thought of nothing else; as you concentrated and focused, your awareness merged with the activity.

Flow is a source of mental energy that accesses positive neural pathways. With flow activities, your mind is fully occupied with one enjoyable activity; negative thoughts do not enter into your head.

In his book *Finding Flow,* Professor Mihaly Csikszentmihalyi says that the mind 'with nothing to do, begins to follow random patterns, usually stopping to consider something painful or disturbing'. However, a mind in a state of flow is so engaged there is no room for negative thoughts.

Where to find flow

Creative interests. Photography, painting, calligraphy, sewing and embroidery. Whatever it is, for many people, a creative activity is a perfect place to completely switch off from everyday concerns.

Sports activities. Tennis, football or bowling; whatever it is, everything in sport happens in the moment. No time to think about anything else because you've got to keep your eye on the ball!

Pilates, yoga, swimming, rock climbing. Concentrating on each individual movement focuses your mind on the movements and the possibility of achieving.

Sing and dance to music. Join a choir or dance class, sing and dance along to your favourite tunes in the kitchen. You'll become immersed in the music and unaware of anything else.

Games and puzzles. It is easy to enter into a state of flow with card and board games, computer games, jigsaws, crosswords and sudoku, because they have goals and rules that make it possible for you to be involved without worrying about what should be done, and how. You can simply focus on the involvement/taking part.

Novels and films. It could be a gripping thriller, science fiction or a clever comedy. Whatever the genre, as events unfold, you become lost in the story.

What are the activities that you enjoy? What hobbies, sports, interests? These are activities with which you can experience flow; they keep you so absorbed that not only can you not dwell on negative thoughts, you're creating positive thoughts. It's a win–win situation!

Having a positive outlook is a choice. You can choose thoughts that throw a constructive light on ordinary, everyday situations as well as difficult situations, and generally colour your day with brighter, more hopeful approaches to the things you do.

> Genius is the ability to renew one's emotions in daily experience.
> Paul Cézanne

By choosing to take a positive outlook on life, you can begin to shift out of an unhelpful frame of mind and see life as filled with possibilities and solutions instead of worries and difficulties.

Key points

- In the context of emotional intelligence, positive thinking encourages you to acknowledge – rather than deny, ignore or avoid – feelings such as jealousy, disappointment, guilt, anxiety and so on. You can then look for and respond to the positive message the emotion is communicating to you.

- In difficult situations, acknowledge – rather than deny, ignore or avoid – the difficulties, and then move on to focusing on the good things. Try to see the best in other people, and view yourself, your emotions and your abilities in a positive light.

- The way you think – whether you are more inclined to be a negative or a positive thinker – is related to your 'explanatory style'. Your explanatory style helps you make sense of the events and experiences in your life.

- You can train your brain to think more positively by giving it lots of opportunities to think more positively; keeping an open mind, for example, imagining positive outcomes, identifying three good things at the end of each day and engaging in activities that give you a sense of flow.

- Making a habit of these positive activities is what reinforces the neural pathways that can really help to establish a positive mindset.

- Like anything else that's practised and constantly repeated, frequently thinking in positive ways can, in time, become automatic: it can become a habit. A positive habit.

PART THREE

Putting It into Practice

7
Manage Worry and Anxiety

What is anxiety?

Sitting an exam, public speaking, driving somewhere new or starting a job are all common sources of anxiety for many of us.

Anxiety is a response to a future event; something that you fear will or might happen, where you don't know how or if you will be able to cope. Anxiety can be based on a past experience. If you have no experience of a situation, you have no idea how it will turn out. But it's also the case that if you *have* experienced a situation in the past and found it difficult and distressing, you may be anxious about facing a similar situation again in case it brings up the same difficult feelings.

Like all emotions, anxiety can have a positive intent; feeling nervous before an exam or giving a presentation, for example, can prompt you to revise for the exam and rehearse the presentation. However, if the feelings of anxiety overwhelm you – you continually think about the worst that could happen, your stomach is in knots and negative thoughts dominate your mind – your ability to concentrate and do well may suffer.

The good news is there are ways to help you manage a spiral of unhelpful thoughts and difficult feelings.

Manage the physical feelings

Shallow breathing, a feeling of dread in the pit of your stomach, 'wired' feelings of tension. These are some of the physical feelings that come with anxiety.

A simple, effective way to manage the physical effects of anxiety is with your breathing.

Try this:

- Stop breathing for five seconds (to 'reset' your breath).
- Next, breathe in slowly for three seconds (count them) and then breathe out more slowly – for five seconds (count them). Be aware that it's the out breath that will slow everything down.

Consciously thinking about your breathing can help divert your thoughts away from whatever it is that you're anxious about.

When you're feeling anxious or stressed, your body releases stress hormones, such as adrenaline and cortisol. These contribute towards physical symptoms such as an increased heart rate. If there's nothing you can do about the cause of your anxiety, those hormones can keep you feeling agitated for quite some time.

Doing something physical can be helpful. It relieves tension, uses up adrenaline and can distract you from those worrying thoughts. You don't have to go for a long run, or visit the gym. A good, steady walk or housework – cleaning the bathroom or kitchen, vacuuming, making beds, cleaning windows and so on – can be just as effective.

Manage your thoughts – think positive

Negative thinking is an inherent part of anxiety. Anxious thoughts take on a life of their own – crowding out any other thoughts.

What to do? Rather than try to suppress or ignore them, start by acknowledging them. Simply say to yourself: 'I'm feeling anxious.'

When you're anxious about something, it can help to confront what the worst end result could be. Then move on to what your options are to minimise or manage the worst case scenario.

For example, supposing you're concerned about driving somewhere new. What's the problem? What are you worried about? What's the worst that can happen? That you'll get horribly lost? Drive round and round in circles, run out of petrol and be stranded?

Rather than be consumed by worried, anxious thoughts about what might happen, turn your mind to finding solutions to whatever it is you think might happen. Worry and anxiety involve your mind going over and over the same problems. Thinking about your options, solutions and a plan to deal with what you're worried might happen can make a big difference in calming a ruminative mind.

There are four steps to take:
1. Identify the specific problem.
2. Identify options and possible solutions.
3. Choose one of the options or solutions.
4. Plan how to carry out the option.

So, once you have identified what, specifically, you're worried about, write down the possible ways you can minimise or manage the problem. Don't feel that you have to find a perfect solution, just identify what you *can* change, rather than aspects of the situation that are beyond your control. After you've decided which option to take, make a plan of action.

So, if you're concerned about driving somewhere new, your options might include using a sat nav, using a map, taking a friend, making sure your phone is charged, leaving in plenty of time.

Once you have a plan and start thinking of positive ways to manage the problem, you'll feel less worried. This is because you'll be doing something positive – something that helps you manage your emotions. You'll be able to replace your negative thinking with more hopeful, positive thoughts.

Try this: write it down

Writing down the problem and the potential solutions on paper or on your phone can be helpful. Then, any time you start to worry, you can look at your plan for dealing with the potential difficulty.

It will read as sound reassurance to prevent the cycle of ruminative worrying. Furthermore, if you find yourself worrying you can say: 'Stop! I have a plan!' Then look at that written plan and keep your thoughts on that. Rather than visualising disaster, visualise a positive outcome – create images for yourself where you see yourself coping. You *do* have a choice – visualise coping or visualise not coping.

You can also use a positive affirmation. Tell yourself: 'I will manage. I can cope!'

Learn from experience

If you have experienced a difficult situation in the past and are anxious about facing similar situations again, think about what you *learned* from that past situation. What did you learn that you can use to make the next experience a better one?

For example, if you did get lost last time you drove somewhere new, what did you learn from that? Look for something new and helpful that you can do next time. Know that you *can* make it different from last time. Again, visualise a positive outcome: see yourself coping. That's emotionally intelligent!

Manage your behaviour

Another way to manage worry and anxiety is to divert your thoughts to another activity – something you enjoy; something constructive (not destructive, like smoking and drinking) that you know requires your mind's attention and stops you getting caught up in your worries.

Identify for yourself activities that you can turn to when you want to switch off from worrying; something that you can dip into for 10 minutes or immerse yourself in for an hour. Something that keeps you focused and engaged; a 'flow activity'. It could be a riveting novel, a crossword or sudoku, a game of tennis or a short yoga sequence, anything that makes it difficult for your mind to wander off or for thoughts about the past or future to find their way into your head. You could do something for someone else; turning your thoughts and efforts to someone else will be appreciated by the other person and give your mind a break.

Of course, it is possible that whatever you do to distract yourself, your mind may keep wandering back to your worries. But if a worrying thought does enter your mind, acknowledge it, let it pass and then return to what you were doing.

Realise that worrying is a choice and do something better with your time. You don't have to feed your worry. When you notice that worries are swirling in your head, focus on another activity.

It might help to write down your worries. Writing down thoughts, fears and worries about the future is a good way to empty your mind. If you have a specific thought bothering you, you can write it down and then observe it. Literally.

When my friend Katya is fretting about something – particularly something that she can't do anything about – she types her worries in an email to herself. She sends it, reads it and deletes it. She tells me that doing this helps her to feel that she's 'dumped' whatever is worrying her – in the trash! She then turns to a different activity.

Communicate: talk about it

Talking to a friend or family member about what's making you anxious can help. You may find that they have experienced a similar problem and can offer advice; or can help you to see what your options are or what the solution is. Often, just having someone listen to you and showing that they care helps in itself.

Voicing your worries can take away a lot of their scariness. If you can't talk to a partner, friend or family member, call a helpline. If it's a specific issue – a health issue of your own or someone you're close to – Google a relevant organisation for their helpline number. For example, Macmillan for support and advice related to cancer http://macmillan.org.uk; or for mental health issues, www.mind.org.uk; and if you are in despair, the Samaritans (08457 90 90 90, open 24 hours a day).

Managing other people's anxiety: how can you help?

Often, if you realise that someone else is worried – one of your children, a friend or a colleague, for example – your reaction may be to simply reassure them by saying: 'everything will be fine', or 'don't worry about it, it's nothing'. You may think you're being helpful, and to an extent you *are* reassuring them, but the other person may also feel that you're shutting them down.

It can help if you are able to think about how *you* feel when you are worried or anxious. Don't, though, assume that your experience of being worried about something is the same as theirs. Use empathy as your starting point only. Don't say: 'Oh, I know exactly how you feel.'

Use active listening. Focus on what the other person is telling you. Gently ask questions and summarise to make sure you have understood what they have told you.

149

On the one hand you need to understand and accept how the other person is feeling. But on the other hand, it can be helpful to encourage them to manage their anxiety. Help the other person to use some of the techniques above to manage their thoughts, feelings and behaviour.

Be assertive: set limits, negotiate and compromise

Be careful not to be caught up in the other person's anxiety – don't make their situation your own.

For example, Daisy's mother Pat is 75 years old. Recently she has started to feel hesitant about driving. Pat and Daisy planned to meet Pat's sister for lunch – a route that Pat has driven many times before.

A week before the lunch date, Pat phoned to tell Daisy she was worried and anxious about driving to her sister's. Pat asked Daisy to pick her up. This would've meant a lengthy round trip for Daisy. Daisy said she understood that her Mum might be anxious about driving anywhere new, but Pat was driving somewhere she's driven many times before. Daisy gently declined to collect Pat.

Pat replied that she might, then, cancel the lunch. Instead of relenting, Daisy thought about what the options were. 'How about I meet you at the retail park – you leave your car there, and I'll drive us from there?' Pat felt she could manage that, and she agreed with Daisy's suggestion.

While giving in to anxious requests can keep the peace in the short term, in the long run it feeds into the cycle of anxiety.

You need to set some limits. Setting limits is not always easy, but it helps stop you becoming entangled in the other person's worries. Limits give you the ability to step back and think about how best you can help someone else to manage their anxiety.

Key points

- Anxiety is a response to a future event; an event that you fear will or might happen, where you don't know how or if you will be able to cope.
- Like all emotions, anxiety can have a positive intent; prompting you to take action to minimise the possibility of the worst from happening.
- When you notice that anxious thoughts are swirling in your head, stressing and upsetting you, know that you *can* do something about it.
- Strategies to manage your thoughts, behaviour and the physical feelings can help you manage a spiral of unhelpful thoughts and difficult feelings.
- You can help someone else to manage their anxiety by listening to them, showing empathy, reassuring and encouraging them to positively manage their thoughts, feelings and behaviour.
- Do though, have limits. Be careful not to be caught up in the other person's anxiety; don't make their situation your own.

8
Managing Anger

Most of us know what it feels like to be overcome by emotions such as anger, guilt and jealousy; they are a normal part of our range of emotions. For some of us, though, there are times when anger can be destructive and do more harm than good. Either we give full vent to our anger, or we try and suppress it and pretend it's not there. If you want to learn to manage anger more effectively, you will need to rethink your usual reactions towards people and situations and take more responsibility for your thoughts and actions.

What is anger?

Anger can be seen as a reaction to an unmet expectation or need. For example, suppose you *expect* that someone should phone you if they are going to be more than 10 minutes late. When they still haven't arrived after 20 minutes, and they haven't phoned or texted, and you can't reach them either, *and* it's the second time this month that they've arrived late . . . you may well be angry. Your heart rate increases, you feel tense and start thinking angry thoughts. You might respond in an aggressive way – berating your friend; or in a passive aggressive way – with sarcasm or sulking.

Another example would be if you were angry with a colleague for failing to have done his share of a project that should be completed the next day. You asked him to get it completed, he agreed, so you believed and expected him to do what he said he'd do. You feel 'wronged'. 'It's his job' you think. 'He's let me down.' 'Bastard!' Your breathing becomes more rapid and you are feeling tense. Again, your response might not be helpful.

Whether it's an unreliable colleague, a friend who is always late, a referee who doesn't call fouls on the opposing team, your teenager's messy bedroom or cold callers, there's a wide variety of situations and other people's behaviour that can 'make' each of us angry. Perhaps your anger can be triggered by friends and family when they let you down or don't show appreciation for something you've done for them. Maybe you get angry with strangers (road rage), social and political issues or things that aren't working as they should.

Sometimes, your anger might build; a confusing mixture of feelings – hurt, frustration, disappointment. Other times, a situation occurs which makes you angry immediately. Either way, anger can easily turn to rage, *blinding* rage (so called because you can't even see), and before you know it, you're saying or doing something that makes everything worse.

As well as different people and events triggering your anger, the intent of the person behind the event will play a part in your response. You might be angry with your friend for being late, but what if you knew that she'd been mugged, had her phone stolen and couldn't contact you? What if you knew that your colleague didn't complete the work because his wife gave birth last evening? Or the driver who cut you up was trying to make it to the hospital with his son who was having an asthma attack? Would your response be different? In a second, your brain determines if the trigger justifies anger.

Like all emotions, anger has three aspects: a thinking part, a feeling part and a behavioural part.

The thinking part involves your thoughts, beliefs and expectations. With the friend who has turned up late again, for example, you might be thinking: 'Late again. And she doesn't even phone to let me know. She's got no consideration. As usual, she's only thinking of herself.'

In cartoons, when a character gets angry, steam comes out their ears, their eyes bulge, their body swells up and turns red. Although it's not as entertaining to watch in real life, anger causes physical effects in us as well: increased heart rate; faster, more shallow breathing; sweating, flushing or paling; tensing up.

You may turn your angry thoughts and feelings into action by berating the person for not phoning; even becoming abusive. Or you may suppress your angry thoughts – bury them and not acknowledge them.

The physical effects of anger are there to motivate us to do something; to make 'right' a 'wrong'. But for this to happen, you have to express your anger appropriately. You can't always control the situation you're in or how it makes you feel, but you *can* manage how you express your anger. And you *can* express your anger without being verbally or physically abusive. Even though it doesn't feel like it at the time, you do have a *choice* about how to respond.

How to manage anger

Manage the physical feelings

The problem is, when you are angry, the emotional part of your brain – the amygdala – is on such high alert, it's almost impossible for the reasoning, thinking part of your mind to get a word in edgeways! Too often you may feel the need to act on it, but later, wish you'd waited.

Emotions say hurry. Wisdom says wait.

Engage the thinking, reasoning part of your brain

When you're angry, if you really need to, you *can* still engage the thinking part of your brain.

Learn to recognise your physical warning signs of anger. Perhaps your voice rises, you feel your breathing speeding up and your body gets tense. Maybe your jaw tightens and you feel your heart pounding.

You need to bring those feelings down until they have less of a physical grip on you.

- Take some deep breaths. Deep, slow breathing helps bring your heart rate back down. One technique is to breathe out for longer than you breathe in, and then relax as you breathe out. So, breathe in for three seconds (count them). Then breathe out for five seconds (count them). Do this for two minutes. Just having to think about and count those three seconds in then five seconds out will also help engage your brain; you think of nothing but your breathing.

- Recite the alphabet backward. Or count backwards from 50. Or recall what you had for breakfast, lunch and dinner yesterday. Doing any of these things can help divert your thinking.
- Let off steam. Ask yourself: 'Am I so angry I can't think?' And: 'Do I want to lash out; verbally or physically?' If the answer to either of these is yes, then you need to remove yourself and go somewhere to calm down. Go for a run or brisk walk, a shower or bath, listen and sing along to some loud heavy rock, scream or swear where it will not alarm anyone. Whatever works for you.

These techniques can help you approach the situation with a clearer head. You can get yourself completely wound up or you can bring yourself down into a calmer place. You have a choice.

If you are patient in one moment of anger, you will escape a hundred days of sorrow.

Chinese proverb

Of course, there are times when you can't confront whatever triggered your anger. It may be impossible, let's say, to track down a reckless driver who pulled out on you. When you can't do this, you have to find helpful ways to get your body to exit its angry state. Use some of the techniques I've just mentioned. Another way to let off steam – particularly when you can't confront the person or situation that triggered it – is simply to call a friend. Warn them that you're angry and ask if they'd mind listening to you rant about it for a few minutes. Doing this can be very helpful!

Sometimes your anger may be triggered unexpectedly – one minute you were fine, then something happens that immediately makes you see red. Other times, you can experience your anger slowly building. When anger builds in this way, the more aware you are of the warning signs, the more likely you can – and must – take effective steps to manage the associated thoughts and physical feelings before they increase to a point where you can no longer engage your brain.

Act as if you have chosen it

Changing how you think – the cognitive aspect of your anger – can be an effective way of managing it. One way to do this is to *act as if you have chosen it*. What I mean by this is that instead of seeing the situation as something that someone or something has imposed on you, see it as a challenge you have *chosen* to engage with.

George is an adult education tutor. He was told by his manager that instead of setting homework for his students, all work had to be completed and assessed in class. At first, George was angry – 'as if I don't have enough to fit in during a lesson'. Later that day, though, he started to reframe the situation – 'if I'd *chosen* to do this, to cut down on the reading and marking of students' work at home, I would find ways to make it work'.

'Reframing' – changing the way you think – can give you a different perspective and a sense of control. So instead of getting all het up and overwhelmed by angry thoughts, turn the situation on its head and try to identify the positives.

What, you might ask, is positive about someone berating you about your driving, for example? Well, when that happened to me, I decided to *'act as if I'd chosen it'* – as if I'd asked the other person for their opinion. In other words, I reframed the situation.

Another example I often use to explain the concept of 'act as if you'd chosen it' is: if another driver cutting you up had been part of a computer driving game, would the same incident have enraged you or would you have seen it as a challenge to skilfully negotiate? Most likely, you would have seen it as a challenge to overcome. And when you had successfully managed the hazard, you would high-five your games partner and congratulate yourself on having avoided disaster!

Reframing won't make a bad situation go away, but it will help you to manage it. You can practise reframing by thinking of past situations where you've got angry. How could you, with hindsight, have reframed the situation?

How and what you think shapes your emotional response to things. For example, if you see something as being 'infuriating', then you will have a specific emotional response to that person or situation. If you change your approach and see the same situation or person as a 'challenge', then your emotional response also changes.

Following these tips won't mean you never get angry, but it should help you manage your anger more constructively and feel better about yourself. Know that it is possible to train yourself to think and feel differently before you respond.

Respond assertively

Once you've calmed down enough to engage your brain, you can use anger in a constructive way, to behave and communicate assertively. First, though, you need to think through your response.

Think about what you do and don't want to happen. Do you just want to let someone know you are angry – or do you want something to change? Of course, you want your friend to be more considerate and to turn up on time. And sure, you want your colleague to have completed the work. But that didn't happen. So, what can *you* do about that?

Think of potential solutions before responding. This is also an opportunity to engage the thinking part of your brain and start thinking of how you might respond – but without responding yet. Ask yourself: What can I do? Think of at least two things. For example, with your colleague who has failed to complete the work; in this situation your options might be to berate them, or reorganise your day so that you can work together to complete the work, or ask someone else to help out, or ask your manager for a solution.

Consider the consequences of each solution. This is where you think about what is likely to result from each of the different solutions you came up with. For example, berating your colleague might escalate the problem. But then it could be just the thing to drive home the message concerning how unacceptable his inaction is!

Ask yourself: What's my best choice? By the time you've thought it through, you're probably past having a go at the other person. Asking someone else to help or reorganising your work might be a good way forward. Then, after the work has been completed, you might also choose to talk to your manager about the situation.

Check your body language. If you decide to tell the other person how you feel, before you say anything, check your body language; it won't be easy, but try and focus on a couple of things that will help keep you feeling in control. For example:

- stand or sit straight – spread your weight evenly on both legs;
- keep your head level;
- keep your hands by your sides.

What to say

Once you have thought about what you want to say, talk to the other person sooner rather than later. Don't think about it for so long that your anger builds up. Using assertiveness, you're looking to address the situation and communicate your thoughts about it clearly. Here's how to do that.

Be specific. For example, say 'I feel angry because . . .'. Use 'I' statements, rather than a 'you' statement: '*You* always turn up late and never text me to let me know you're delayed.' 'You' statements blame the other person. When the other person is blamed, they will attack back, defend themselves or withdraw. Successful 'I' statements open up discussion: 'I feel annoyed that I have to wait for you to arrive and that you don't let me know you're going to be late. Could you phone me or at least switch your phone on so I can reach you?' Or: 'I'm feeling annoyed that you haven't done your share of this project.' Using 'I' avoids blaming anyone, and the other person is less likely to feel attacked. You can choose whether or not to tell the other person how you're feeling.

Keep to the point. As well as being direct and specific, keep to the point. Don't drag up past crimes or irrelevant issues. You'll only confuse the situation.

Listen to the other person's response and try to see their point of view. Reflective listening can help here – by paraphrasing what the other person says, you slow the situation down, which helps take the heat out of the matter and helps lead to solutions to the problem.

Find a solution. If the other person doesn't do what you want, what will you do? What you don't want to do is think in terms of retribution and punishments. Instead, think about what *you* can do – what solution you can come up with to manage the situation and your feelings. For example, you might decide that the solution with your friend who is always late is to only leave your house to meet her once she's confirmed that she has in fact left her house and is on her way. Put it nicely – in a calm, friendly voice suggest: 'It'll help stop me getting so wound up and take the pressure off you if you message me when you're leaving your house.'

Be aware that being aggressive can get in the way of communicating what you are angry about. People stop listening to you and focus on your anger instead. If you are able to express your anger by talking in an assertive way, it will produce better results for both of you. Use anger to put an end to the problems, not your relationships.

If, on the other hand, you often suppress your anger, know that it will take time, effort and practice to get into the habit of expressing anger in a direct way that explains why you are annoyed. But it *can* be achieved!

Check your progress. After you've responded and the situation is over, *ask yourself*: How did I do? Did things work out as I would have liked them to? If not, why not? Taking some time to reflect on how things worked out after it's all over helps you learn about yourself and what does and doesn't work for you. Give yourself a pat on the back if the solution you chose worked out well. If it didn't, think about what you would have done differently, so that if you're in a similar situation again, you already have an alternative course of action.

Quite simply, you need to explain how you feel and be prepared to find a solution. This might mean standing your ground, but it may also mean being prepared to compromise, negotiate and find alternative ways forward.

Managing someone else's anger

Remember, anger happens when the expectations and beliefs a person has about a situation and the way things 'should' be differs from what actually happens. The person sees that difference as a *negative* thing and they feel wronged, offended, threatened or attacked in some way.

When a person is angry and is openly rude and abusive, it can be really difficult to manage your own feelings. However, there are ways to avoid reacting emotionally to someone else's anger and manage how and what they're feeling. You'll need to use listening skills and take an assertive approach.

When a person is angry, it's easy for them to become unreasonable and illogical because the anger has taken over their rational mind. Their ability to think in a calm, reasonable way has been switched off. It's as if you are communicating with the emotion, not the person.

An angry person needs to let it all out, so don't say anything until they have finished. Listen without interrupting to defend yourself or disagreeing, because the moment that you oppose what they are saying, you're adding fuel to the fire.

Acknowledge what they are saying with the minimum of minimal encouragers; nodding your head and uttering things like 'uh huh' and 'mmm' and 'oh'.

When you *do* respond, lower the pitch of your voice and speak more slowly. You may need to start by repeating back some of the main points or comments that have been made such as: 'Ok, you're saying that you don't like it when . . .' or 'You feel that this is not what you wanted or asked for. . .'.

Ask questions so that you are clear about

- what their expectations were;
- what they want to happen next – what would put things right; what solutions they might have.

Don't think that asking them what they want to happen next will mean they have to tell you. But asking the angry person what they now want can help you know what their expectations are.

Then, state how *you* feel and how *you* see the situation. You might disagree with their perspective and what they expect. But you may agree with their point of view and, if their anger is directed at you, apologise and explain what you can do to rectify the situation.

Only take responsibility for your own actions. You are not responsible for anyone else's behaviour or for the emotions someone else is feeling. You are not to blame if they choose to be angry or upset with you, someone or something else. They need to manage their own feelings and reactions.

You can, however, help or exacerbate the situation through your responses. By using reflective listening, you show that you're taking the other person seriously and you slow the situation down.

When people are in conflict, they often contradict each other, denying each other's view of a situation. Both sides get defensive, and they will either lash out or withdraw and say nothing more. However, if they feel that the other person is really listening, they are likely to explain what they feel, what they do and don't want and why.

If both parties to a conflict do this, the chances of being able to reach a solution are higher. And that's emotionally intelligent!

However, do not remain with the other person if they are so angry that they are confusing or scaring you. Say: 'I know you're furious about what happened but I'm feeling confused and scared. I need to take some time out. Let's talk about it later.'

Key points

- Anger can be seen as a reaction to an unmet expectation or need. Anger can motivate you to put right a wrong. But anger can be destructive and do more harm than good.
- When you're angry, the emotional part of your brain – the amygdala – is on such high alert, it's almost impossible for the reasoning, thinking part of your mind to get a word in edgeways!

- When you know what's likely to trigger anger in you, and when you are aware of the warning signs, the more likely you can – and must – take steps to manage the associated thoughts and physical feelings before they increase to a point where you can no longer engage your brain.

- There are techniques that can help you engage the rationalising, reasoning part of your brain and approach the situation with a clearer head. You can get yourself completely wound up, or you can bring yourself down to a calmer place. You have a choice.

- Once you're calm enough to engage your brain, you can use anger in a constructive way, to behave and communicate assertively.

- Following the ideas and suggestions in this chapter for managing anger's physical and cognitive aspects won't mean you never get angry, but it should help you manage your behaviour and responses more constructively.

- Check your progress; reflecting on how things worked out after it's all over helps you learn about yourself and what does and doesn't work for you.

- If you are confronted with someone else's anger, know that when a person is angry, it's easy for them to become unreasonable and illogical because the anger has taken over their rational mind.

- You can help or exacerbate the situation through your responses. By using reflective listening, you show that you're taking the other person seriously and you slow the situation down.

- An angry person needs to let it all out, so don't say anything until they have finished. Listen without interrupting to defend yourself or disagreeing.

- When they've said their piece, acknowledge what they said. State how *you* feel and how *you* see the situation. Speak calmly and look for solutions.
- Only take responsibility for your own actions. You are not responsible for how the other person expresses their anger. Do not remain with the other person if they are so angry that they are confusing or scaring you.

9
Understanding and Managing Disappointment

The American talk show host Oprah Winfrey was fired from her first job as a TV news presenter for becoming 'too emotionally involved' in the news stories. Early in *his* career Walt Disney was fired by a newspaper editor because he 'lacked imagination' and 'had no good ideas'; Albert Einstein failed his college entrance exam and the hugely successful basketball player Michael Jordan was once cut from his high school basketball team. From Nobel Prize winners to talk show hosts, these figures all had their share of disappointments.

Whether you didn't get the job, flat or house, had your holiday plans cancelled, your team lost or you didn't get offered a place on a TV talent show, disappointment can be a difficult emotion.

What is disappointment?

Disappointment is a feeling of loss; the sadness that occurs when your expectations or hopes fail to materialise. Disappointment differs from regret in that with regret, you focus on the personal choices that contributed to a 'wrong' outcome. But with disappointment, you focus on the outcome itself.

Even if you're trying to forget about it, disappointment can hover at the front of your mind and niggle at the back.

Manage disappointment

Unlike anger, which often needs reining in, with disappointment, you really do need to sit with it; to experience the feeling.

A few years ago, a keenly anticipated family trip was cancelled due to weather conditions. I was hugely disappointed. 'I can't believe it . . . I'm so disappointed . . . I was so looking forward to this . . . I can't believe it' I kept saying. After an hour my teenage son told me: 'It's happened. There's nothing you can do about it.' 'I know,' I replied. 'I will get over it. But for a bit longer I just have to keep saying how upset and disappointed I am. I'll soon get bored with it and move on. But for now I'm just trying to take it in.' I knew that I just needed some time to adjust and accept the reality of the situation.

Some of us are not very good at fully experiencing disappointment without trying to speed up the process.

Children cry until the emotion runs out and they're ready to move on. That's not to suggest that you wallow in it for long periods whenever you've been disappointed, but do resist any pressure to 'just get over it'.

Acknowledge what you are feeling and take your time

What you're feeling is OK. Take some time to just sit with disappointment and experience it without burying it or moving to fix or change it.

If you can give yourself some time and space to experience your feelings of disappointment, it becomes easier to accept;

to acknowledge that what has happened has happened and nothing can change that.

Be assertive with yourself: move on

At some point though – sooner rather than later – you are going to have to move on. How will you know when it's time to move on? By asking yourself: 'What have I got to gain by continuing to dwell on this?' One of the main reasons many of us find it difficult to move on is because we're focusing on what we've lost; the lost opportunity. In order to let go and move on, you need to focus on your next move – on something positive.

My husband is a football fan – he supports Brighton and Hove Albion. If his team doesn't win, like many football supporters, he doesn't remain disappointed for long. Why? He's moved on to thinking about the next game and the opportunities it will present. In fact, all sports fans are examples of people who must cope with disappointment on a regular basis; someone will always win and someone will always lose. As Martin Luther King once said; 'We must accept finite disappointment but never lose finite hope.'

How to move on from disappointment

It's an emotionally intelligent person who realises that being stuck in disappointment gets them nowhere. You must make a decision that you are going to move forward. It won't happen automatically. Here's how to move on.

(Continued)

Think positive. Sometimes a series of disappointments can leave you feeling that you're unlucky, that things never go well for you. However, it *is* possible to find something positive in a disappointment. Take, for example, the contestants on TV talent shows. When they get voted off, despite their disappointment they always express what a privilege and wonderful experience it has been to take part.

You can always draw out something good from a disappointment. Do look for just one positive aspect of what did or didn't happen.

Find the lesson. Think about a time that you suffered a disappointment. What was it that you learnt; what lessons were present? Did you even stop to reflect on this? Think about what you've learnt from that experience and would now do differently in a similar situation.

Have a Plan B. You can mitigate – lessen the distress – against future disappointments. When you're planning to do something or hoping for something to happen, have a Plan B: an alternative course of action in case things don't work out. You've probably already done this in the past. For example, if you planned an outdoor event – a picnic, for example – you would've had a Plan B in case it rained on the day.

So, knowing that you might not get the job, flat or house, a place on a TV talent show or good weather for an outdoor event, consider back-up plans or a strategy for the next best thing. Then, if things don't work out, refocusing your attention on Plan B will help you manage and lessen the disappointment. Plan B gives you hope; the feeling that what you want can be had or that events can still turn out well.

Any person who has succeeded or achieved something in life has faced some disappointments. They learn from their disappointments and move forward. And sometimes that may be in a different direction.

Gain perspective. Even the smallest disappointments can seem monumental at first. But once you have acknowledged how you feel, take a step back and look at the larger picture. How much of an effect is this disappointment going to have on you next week, next month or next year?

Share your feelings. Talk it through with a supportive friend, family member or colleague; someone who'll sympathise, empathise and might offer a different way of looking at the situation.

How to manage someone else's disappointment

When it comes to managing someone else's disappointment, what matters most is how well you listen and respond to the other person.

Be prepared for strong emotions. Acknowledge those emotions. Unless the disappointment affects you directly too, try not to make their situation your own and get too emotional yourself.

Acknowledge their disappointment. You can't fix their broken phone or laptop, get them the job, flat, place on the course or rearrange their holiday plans for them. But you can acknowledge the other person's disappointment; your response should reflect your understanding of how the other person feels. So, you might say: 'I'm sorry you're so upset. I can see this makes things difficult for you.' Or: 'I can see this is disappointing for you.'

Avoid saying: 'I know just how you feel.' Or: 'Try not to let it get you down too much.' Although you might mean well, the other person may feel that actually, you *don't* understand or that you're trying to move off the subject.

Suggest a way forward. When it's appropriate, say something positive. This is *not* to imply that things aren't that bad. The reason to include something positive is so that the other person has something positive to grasp. For example: 'You've got another job interview coming up next week. Can I help you prepare for that?'

State what, if anything, you can do to help, or ask: 'Is there anything I can do?' Suggest possible actions, directions or ideas on what steps to take next. Focus on what can be done rather than what can't be done.

Key Points

- Disappointment is a feeling of loss; the sadness that occurs when your expectations or hopes fail to materialise.
- Give yourself some time and space to experience your feelings of disappointment, to acknowledge and accept that what has happened *has* happened and can't be changed.
- If you're finding it difficult to move on, ask yourself what you have to gain by continuing to dwell on the disappointment. Get some perspective. Ask yourself how much of an effect the disappointment is going to have on you, next week, next month or next year.
- Look for one positive aspect of what did or didn't happen. Think about what you've learnt from the

experience; what would you now do differently in a similar situation?

- Mitigate against disappointment. In future, when you're planning or hoping for something to happen, have a Plan B. Then, if things don't work out, you will have an alternative course of action to focus on.
- When it comes to managing someone else's disappointment, what matters most is how well you listen and respond to the other person.
- Acknowledge the other person's disappointment; suggest a way forward and say what, if anything, you can do to help.

10
Understanding and Managing Bullying

Identifying and understanding bullying

A bully is a person who deliberately badgers, domineers and intimidates others.

Why does a person behave as a bully? Several reasons. A bully might behave as they do as a result of differences they perceive between you. These differences can include appearance, gender, family culture, nationality, religion, behaviour, sexual orientation or abilities. It may be because you're good at what you do or not very good at what you do. It could be because of how well liked you are by others – colleagues, clients, customers, friends and family. It could be the other person is jealous of a relationship between other people or envious of your talents, abilities, circumstances or possessions. Maybe they just don't like you. Whatever the reason, they are controlling and abusive.

Bullying can take many forms including:

- teasing
- coercing
- humiliating
- tyrannising and terrorising

- threatening
- spreading rumours
- name calling
- derogatory remarks.

Bullying can happen face to face, behind your back and online; communicating insulting, offensive, abusive messages through texts, emails, social media, phone calls and so on.

Direct, overt bullying is obvious and aggressive. Indirect bullying is more underhand and less detectable – it includes spreading rumours, excluding a person, setting them up to fail, manipulating or undermining them. Indirect bullying uses passive aggressive behaviour.

Bullies come in all shapes and sizes. Bullying can happen anywhere: at home, at work, school, college, travelling to and from school, in sports teams, between neighbours.

How come a bully seems to know exactly how to get at you? Do they know how much distress they are causing?

It may be that the bully actually has well-developed empathy and emotional intelligence. They know how to use and manage other people's emotions, but instead of using their abilities in a positive way, they do it in an abusive way. This type of bully is tuned in to what gets a reaction. As soon as you blush, get defensive or you react in any way other than with a casual shrug or a witty remark then they know they have got to you. One form of bullying, internet 'trolling', is often done to see how people will react. Trolls get their excitement from opposing reactions, which they can escalate.

The science

Jean Decety is a neuroscientist at the University of Chicago who studies empathy. He's interested in how we share and understand the feelings of another person.

Decety says that for most people, seeing others in pain makes you connect with that person's pain, and it's an unpleasant experience for you. Witness someone stub their toe, for example, and you wince as you 'feel' their pain.

But the young people in Decety's study in 2008 – young people with a history of aggression – don't experience that empathy.

Decety showed them a video of someone getting hurt. As they watched, MRI scans showed that the areas in the young people's brains that identify pain lit up. They did recognise that others were in pain, but seeing others in distress activated the region of their brains associated with reward.

Decety suggests that while these young people can recognise painful emotions, they don't interpret it as being a bad thing. On the contrary, they see other people's distress as a good thing.

'If you're healthy, you don't like to see people suffering', Decety says. 'But bullies not only don't care, they like it.'

How to manage a bully

Shame, anxiety, embarrassment, guilt and fear are common emotions in response to being bullied. The bully is playing on these emotions – using them as tactics of control. They use deception, amoral behaviour and abuse of power.

Although feelings of shame, guilt, anxiety and so on are painful, remember that they have a positive intent; they are telling you to do something, to take action. And you *must* do something. The bully will not go away; if you make yourself an easy target, you will only encourage the bully.

Don't try and please them, pacify them or ingratiate yourself with them; but don't stay silent either. Staying silent and telling no one simply serves to isolate you while at the same time empowering the bully.

Get help and support. There is no shame or failure in this – the bully is devious, deceptive, evasive and manipulative. He or she is the one who should be feeling guilt and shame. Getting help is the first step to resolving a situation that's not acceptable.

Tell someone you trust. Ask for their support and advice. Ask other people how they'd manage the bully. You don't have to take their advice, but at least see if they've got any useful ideas.

If you feel there is no one to talk to, don't suffer in silence as there *is* help out there. There are also professional organisations that specialise in bullying. For example: Family Lives, www.familylives.org.uk; Young Minds www.youngminds .org.uk; Acas www.acas.org.uk. Go to their websites and put 'bullying' into the search bar.

Why don't other people help?

Sometimes, support from friends, family or colleagues is not forthcoming. If there is an environment or culture within a family, community or organisation that, at best, tolerates bullying, and at worst, simply accepts intimidating, domineering or humiliating behaviour, then you are not in a strong position.

There are two main reasons why others fail to come to the aid of someone being bullied. First, other people may not have the integrity or courage or know how to stand up against bullying and harassment. The bully can create a climate of fear where everybody is afraid to speak out for fear of reprisal.

Second, people don't always recognise the tactics of bullying, especially the use of guilt and sarcasm. Bullies are adept at manipulating other people's perceptions. They know how to encourage a negative view of the other person to instil doubt and suspicion in the minds of everyone else.

Bullies may exert power and control by a combination of selectively withholding information and spreading disinformation. This means others have a distorted picture. They have a picture only of what the bully wants them to see.

It can also be that support is not forthcoming because, sadly, the other people know of no other way of bonding except in the vilification of others; actively joining in with victimising and scapegoating.

Be assertive with yourself

If support is not forthcoming, you might feel that there is no respite and no release from the pressure. If that's the case, do seriously consider leaving the job, the relationship or the social media account. How can this be assertive? Because you are deciding how you feel and deciding what you do and don't want. Then you're taking action. That's assertive. Regard it as a *positive* decision in the face of overwhelming odds which are not of your choosing, nor of your making, and over which you have no control. Walking away is the best thing to do, for in doing so, you regain control. You take away the opportunity for the bully to behave like this towards you.

Imagine, for example, someone is driving really close to you, trying to intimidate you. Why try to block that driver or confront him? You can control the situation more easily than that. How? By pulling over when it's safe to do so and letting the other driver pass.

Refuse to allow your life to be wrecked. Bullies are compulsive in their behaviour; once they start on their target they won't let go.

Bullies are clever, but you can be clever too. Remember, you have a choice about how to respond. What's most important? That you stand your ground or that you keep yourself safe?

Whatever the situation, you need to ask yourself the same question. What's most important? Your job, your health, your mental health, your career, your life, your family? Sure, it can be difficult to walk away from a job or a relationship. But know this: the energy that's draining out of you as a result of this bullying can be used to get a new job or find somewhere else to live or whatever is relevant for you to move away from the bullying. Redirecting that energy is emotionally intelligent; you're using and managing how you feel in a helpful way.

Use positive thinking. Yes, you might have to walk away from a good job/financial stability, but focus on the positive side;

you *will* be able to manage that. What you can't manage is the bully.

Emily's first job after university was as an assistant for a TV production company. Her manager, Joely, was a bully. She bullied everyone.

'For example,' explains Emily, 'if a colleague complimented me on a piece of work I'd done, my manager would tend to avoid engaging with me for the rest of the day.'

Often, Joely would give orders one day, then contradict them the next. When anyone queried her requests and demands, she became aggressive and accused us of deliberately misunderstanding. She dismissed the need to pay us for overtime worked. We were regularly shouted at. After a colleague left, I took over organising a gift voucher for Christmas for the office cleaner. It was, as usual, paid for out of petty cash. Joely reprimanded me for not asking her first and insisted I paid it back out of my own money.

I knew her behaviour wasn't right but it hadn't occurred to me that adults would behave like this (and be allowed to get away with it) in the workplace. I was feeling absolutely miserable.

She was highly critical and often verbally abusive. Joely was in charge and what she said went. If anybody didn't like it they could leave. So I did.'

This same approach of disengaging from a bully also applies to online bullying. Block them and do not read anything they say.

Having walked away from a situation where you've been bullied, you may feel guilty, annoyed or ashamed. Don't make things worse by beating yourself up about it. Instead, reflect on how you could change your response if you came across a bully in future. It makes sense to have some strategies in place to help you manage a bully before they can get started.

Manage a bully assertively

Bullies are only effective when they're on solid ground; ground that you can take away. You can deal with a potential bully if you are prepared to use courage and be assertive.

If someone else is directing intimidating or humiliating behaviour towards you, it's likely you'll feel anxiety, embarrassment or fear. Although these feelings are difficult, they have a positive intent; they are telling you to take action. And you *must* do something; you must nip their behaviour in the bud. If you don't, you will only make yourself an easy target and encourage the bully.

Think clearly. You need to slow everything down so that you can access the rational thinking part of your brain and overcome the emotional part. You can do this by focusing on your breathing (breathe in slowly for three seconds and then breathe out more slowly – for five seconds).

Wear a bracelet or another piece of jewellery that you touch or tug to remind you to engage your brain.

Set limits. Your limits and boundaries can also help you decide what you will do if the other person's behaviour is becoming unreasonable. What are you willing and unwilling to accept from someone else's behaviour?

One way to confront bullying behaviour is to simply and calmly say what you do or don't want to happen. 'Please don't shout at me. Just explain it again.' Or, if someone was making a sarcastic remark about how you should or shouldn't do something, you might respond with: 'Could you please just tell me what you want.'

Decide what the consequence or solution will be if the other person doesn't stop. It's useful to have already decided what steps you are going to take if the bullying behaviour occurs again. We're not talking threats or punishments here. Threats increase the emotional temperature and make an argument more likely. So, remain firm and let them know that you're prepared to take further action if necessary.

For example, if you have a colleague who shouts and is verbally abusive, you might say: 'Either you get a grip and calm down or I'll walk away and we can talk about this when you're calmer.'

Bullies seek out victims who appear weak, so showing you have the courage to speak up will certainly send a clear message that you are strong. In itself, that message may be enough to stop the bully in their tracks. But if it doesn't, you must take courage and follow through with the consequence or solution – in this example, you would walk away.

Practise. You might want to rehearse these steps with a friend so that you are more comfortable responding when the bully attacks. Use assertive body language: if you're trying not to be noticed, you can be sure the bully *will* notice.

(*Continued*)

If you step out boldly you send out a quite different message of confidence. You may not be very confident, but you'll certainly look it. Remember to use just one or two confident actions:

- stand or sit straight;
- keep your head level;
- relax your shoulders;
- spread your weight evenly on both legs;
- if sitting, keep your elbows on the arms of your chair (rather than tightly against your sides);
- make appropriate eye contact;
- lower the pitch of your voice;
- speak more slowly.

If you can just use one or two of those things consistently, your thoughts, feelings and the rest of your behaviour will catch up. It's a dynamic process where small changes in how you use your body can add up to a big change in how you feel, how you behave and the impact you have on other people.

Get help. If you feel there is no one to talk to, remember: you don't have to suffer in silence as there are professional organisations that specialise in advice for anyone who is being bullied. For example, Family Lives, www.familylives.org.uk; Young Minds, www.youngminds.org.uk; Acas, http://acas.org.uk, who provide free and impartial advice for employers and employees. Go to their websites and put 'bullying' into the search bar.

Help someone who is being bullied

There are usually signs and clues that someone is being bullied. You might be afraid that if you do something about it, the bully could pick on you next. But there are things you can do to help.

Start by talking to the person you think is being bullied to find out more about the situation. Find out if they want your help, support or advice. If they do want your help, you could:

Stick up for them. Include the person being bullied into your group. Just doing this will help them feel less isolated. If you witness a bullying behaviour or remark, you might simply say: 'Hey, that's not nice.' Or: 'Hey, that was unnecessary.' If you witness several instances of bullying, tell the bully what the consequences or solution will be if they don't stop. Do, though, take care to ensure that in trying to stick up for the person being bullied, you don't make the situation worse or put yourself in danger.

Practise. Help the person being bullied to practise and role play assertive responses and behaviour.

Look for a Plan B. Help the person being bullied to explore their options if they withdraw from the bully by leaving their job, the relationship or wherever the bullying situation has been occurring.

Get help. There are also professional organisations out there that specialise in advice for anyone who is being bullied – see page 186 for their details.

Respect their position. Be aware that the person you are talking with could be feeling vulnerable and be scared to talk about it. If they resist your enquiries, step back. Simply let that person know you are concerned. And if it's weighing too much on your mind, seek help and advice yourself about what can be done.

Key points

- A bully is a person who deliberately badgers, domineers and intimidates others. For one reason or another, they are manipulative, controlling and abusive.

- Bullying can happen in any setting and can occur face to face, behind your back or online. It might occur in overt, aggressive ways or in less detectable, passive aggressive ways.
- Feelings of shame, guilt, anxiety and so on are telling you to do something: to take action. Don't try and please or pacify the bully or ingratiate yourself with them, but don't stay silent either. Do get help and support.
- However, other people often don't help because you and they are in an environment or culture that encourages, tolerates or simply accepts intimidating, domineering or humiliating behaviour.
- It could be, though, that others don't recognise the tactics of bullying, or don't have the integrity or courage or know how to stand up against bullying and harassment.
- Refuse to allow your life to be wrecked. Bullies are compulsive in their behaviour; once they start on their target they won't let go.
- Before things get worse, get out! Do consider leaving the job, the relationship or the social media account.
- Walking away is the best thing to do, for in doing so, you regain control. You take away the opportunity for the bully to behave like this towards you.
- You can then use the time and energy the stress was taking from you to, for example, get a new job, place to live, relationship and so on. You can manage that. What you can't manage is the bully.
- If you come across a bully in future, you must nip their behaviour in the bud. Have some strategies in place – setting limits, deciding on next steps and solutions and so on – to help you manage them before they can get started.

- You can help someone who is being bullied by – if it's safe – sticking up for them. You could offer to help them to practise assertive responses. You can also help explore their options if they withdraw from the bully by leaving wherever the bullying situation is occurring. Finally, you can help identify further sources of advice and help.

11
Motivating and Inspiring People

If you've ever tried to get someone else to do something – neighbours to help out at a community event, a teenager to tidy their room or a friend to take that job or leave their abusive partner – you'll know that you can't simply order people around and expect them to do what you want. Rather than *make* people do something, you need to take an emotionally intelligent approach: create an environment within which they can, and will, do something of their own free will.

When there's an immediate, specific goal that you want people to achieve or that they themselves want to achieve, you need to motivate them; give them a reason to achieve something. You'll need to engage their *logical, rational reasoning* side.

If you want to *inspire* them, you'll need to spark up their soul and light up their spirit. You'll need to engage their *emotions and imagination*. Often, in any one situation, you'll need to do both; to motivate and inspire.

Motivating and inspiring other people gives you the opportunity to bring out the best in them; to tap into people's best intentions and encourage them to believe 'Yes, I *can* do it!'

Motivating other people

Be clear about what it is you're asking the other person to do. Motivation is all about getting people to take action, so don't be vague about what that action is. For example, instead of just saying 'I want you to tidy your room' say 'I want you to put your dirty clothes in the wash, bring those plates to the kitchen and vacuum your room'.

And, in another example, instead of just saying 'I need you to help out at the village fete', follow that with what, exactly, you'd like them to do. Say, for example, 'I'd like you to run the raffle'. And in a third example, rather than say 'you need to complete all the paperwork for this project', say 'there are three forms that need to be completed'.

Keep it focused; simplify your request and don't ramble on. Make it easy for them to understand.

Other people need to know how much time or effort you're asking for, so you need to be clear about that too. It's easier to ask people to work late one night or even every night for a week than to expect them to work late indefinitely.

Listen to the response. Once you have clearly stated what needs doing, stop talking and listen to the response. If the other person is unsure or resistant, find out what their feelings and concerns are. People are far more willing to cooperate if they feel listened to; that their needs and concerns are acknowledged and addressed. You do not need to agree with what they are thinking and what difficulties they see, but you do need to understand why they feel this way.

Accentuate the positive. Ask questions. Find out what the other person wants. What incentives do they need? Recognise what motivates them. Be willing to hear things that differ from what's motivating to you, or from what you think ought to be motivating to them. Telling someone that if they tidied their room/office/desk, they'd be able to find what they needed more easily might be something *you* see as a benefit. The other person might not see finding things more easily as a benefit at all. Explain how *they* stand to gain and benefit, not you!

> When an actor comes to me and wants to discuss his character, I say 'it's in the script.' If he says 'But what's my motivation?' I say, 'Your salary.
>
> Alfred Hitchcock

Be open to negotiation and compromise. You'll need to be prepared to offer something in return for the other person doing what you want them to do. For example, to the teenager – 'If you tidy your room, I'll give you a lift to the party.' To your neighbour: 'If you could run the raffle, I'll ask someone else to take over from you for an hour so you can have a break.'

Inspiring other people

It's not just motivational speakers, teachers, politicians and preachers whose role it is to motivate and inspire people. With friends and family, at social occasions, at work, in meetings and giving presentations, we all have an opportunity to bring out the best in other people.

Whether it's to win the league this season or to save a community hall or pub from developers who want to turn the building into flats, what inspires people is being able to achieve in areas that are important to them; that, in some way, they have an emotional attachment to.

They are inspired by emotions like excitement, pride, a sense of belonging and the thrill of achievement. Inspiration requires and involves emotion. Inspiring people means that you connect emotionally with them.

Inspiration appeals to people's best intentions, and its underlying, often unspoken message is: 'You can achieve something special. You can realise your potential. You can make a difference for other people and to the world.' Inspiration involves overtly influencing the way people think and feel so that they want to take positive actions. It taps into people's values and desires.

Start by being clear about what exactly the goal is. What you want other people to achieve. Know that you will need to make a clear statement, acknowledge the difficulties, but keep people focused on the prize.

Acknowledge the negative but focus on the positive. Other people need to know what the challenges are, so you will have to be clear about that too. There will always be difficulties – inspiring others means you recognise the difficulties and are clear that they *can* be overcome and you *can* succeed.

If you show doubt, you can easily erode any positive influence you might have instilled.

In his speech, known as 'We Shall Fight on the Beaches', given to Parliament on 4 June 1940, Prime Minister Winston Churchill had to warn of a possible invasion attempt by the Nazis without casting doubt on eventual victory.

Listen to this speech and other inspirational speeches, such as Martin Luther King's 'I Have a Dream' or Colonel Tim Collins' eve-of-battle speech from 2003. You will notice that they do not deny the difficulties – they acknowledge the challenges – but emphasise the positive.

It's not easy – the process of inspiring others comes with no shortage of challenges that need to be faced, either personally or collectively. To manage this, you must always acknowledge the difficulties (otherwise you may be dismissed as an idealist), stay positive and present optimism openly to others no matter what the circumstances are.

If you can support people and encourage them when things are difficult, you'll be inspiring them to see the best in themselves and in the situation. Explain why their contributions help solve problems and contribute to overcoming difficulties. People are more likely to be inspired if they see that their hard work will make a difference.

Suggest, rather than demand. When you're inspiring people, you're not telling them what, specifically, they need to do or giving them precise directions. Instead, inspiration should use suggestion, not demand. The emphasis is on engaging their imaginations and emotions; getting them to visualise what success will look like; showing people what they're capable of becoming or doing.

One way to do this is give examples. So, to inspire people to work together to save their community hall and raise money to refurbish it, generate images in their minds that provide a clear picture of the future; what the hall could look like; what it could offer in the way of facilities. Look beyond the obvious; tell them about the wider reaching impact that extends into the community.

Your aim is to give other people the confidence and belief to achieve their goals.

Our chief want is someone who will inspire us to be what we know we could be.

Ralph Waldo Emerson

Share from your own experience. Overcoming difficulties is a source of inspiration, so if it's relevant, use your experiences to help others. When it's appropriate and relevant, be willing to share your failures as well as your successes. Others will relate to you. They'll understand that they're not the only ones with challenges.

Be the change you want to inspire. Your actions will help to inspire people, so if you want to bring the best out of others, you need to expect the best from yourself.

Inspire yourself. Look for people, ideas, environments and knowledge that you find inspiring and motivating.

And finally, here's an inspiring quote: The author of the book *The Little Prince* wrote: 'If you want to build a ship, don't drum up the men to gather wood, divide the work and give orders. Instead, teach them to yearn for the vast and endless sea.'

Sometimes you need to do both. If you need to enlist and organise people to do a specific task, then you need to motivate them. But if you want to inspire them, you'll need to light up people's desires, emotions and imagination.

Key points

- To motivate someone you need give them a reason to achieve something. You need to engage their logical, rational reasoning side.

- If you want to inspire someone, you need to spark up their soul and light up their spirit. You need to engage their emotions and imagination. Often, in any one situation, you'll need to do both: to motivate and inspire.
- To motivate someone, be clear about what it is you're asking them to do; how much time and effort is required.
- If they are unsure or resistant, find out what their feelings and concerns are. What incentives do they need? They might be different from what you think ought to be motivating to them.
- Be open to negotiation and compromise. Be prepared to offer something in return for the other person doing what you want them to do.
- Inspiration requires and involves emotions; pride and courage, for example. Inspiring people means that you connect emotionally with them.
- Inspiration also involves overtly influencing the way people think and feel so that they want to take positive actions and achieve something that matters to them. It taps into people's values and desires.
- Inspiration should use suggestion not demand. The emphasis is on engaging imaginations and emotions; getting people to visualise what success will look like; showing people what they're capable of becoming or doing.
- Acknowledge the difficulties, but be optimistic; explain that they *can* overcome difficulties and succeed.

About the Author

Gill Hasson is a teacher, trainer and writer. She has 20 years' experience in the area of personal development. Her expertise is in the areas of confidence and self-esteem, communication skills, assertiveness and resilience.

Gill delivers teaching and training for education organizations, voluntary and business organizations and the public sector.

Gill is the author of the best-selling *Mindfulness* and other books on the subjects of resilience, communication skills, assertiveness and emotional intelligence.

Gill's particular interest and motivation is in helping people to realize their potential; to live their best life! You can contact Gill via her website www.makingsenseof.com or email her at gillhasson@btinternet.com

Index

Index

Index

Index

Index

Index